"*Christians and Alcohol: A Scriptural Case for Abstinence* is a must-read for those who truly want to understand the importance of social drinking and the Christian walk. With his usual wit and humor, Dr. Jaeggli discusses modern alcohol usage at both lay and theological levels, making this presentation both enjoyable and academic. In particular, his comprehensive review of the medical facts surrounding drinking alcoholic beverages is accurate and timely, giving a very convincing exposé of the physical, emotional, and spiritual dangers surrounding modern alcohol consumption."

—DANIEL T. BORKERT, MD
Mile High Family Medicine, Lakewood, Colorado

"Dr. Jaeggli is devoted to elevating and applying the Word with exacting rigor, allowing the Scriptures to speak for themselves historically, linguistically, and practically. His arrangement is largely inductive, helping young believers wrestle with the ubiquity and intensity of an issue that has not been faced to the same degree by previous generations. Though the temptations of argumentation are powerful, Dr. Jaeggli takes the reader back to Scripture—the Christian's authority for faith and practice. Read carefully and prayerfully—this volume offers tremendous help to those 'in the world, but not of the world.'"

—STEPHEN JONES, PhD
Former President, Bob Jones University, Greenville, South Carolina

"In this thorough look at a thorny subject, the author takes a strong stand against drinking and supports it from practical, exegetical, historical, medical, and spiritual considerations."

—TOM COLEMAN, PhD
Senior Pastor, Calvary Independent Baptist Church, Huntingdon, Pennsylvania

"Surely this is the 'magnum opus' presenting the case for Christians on the subject of total abstinence from the use of alcoholic beverages. Dr. Jaeggli carefully and systematically exegetes the subject from Scripture; and in addition, so fairly and comprehensively covers the subject medically, historically, and culturally that his facts and logic must give pause to Christians who would consider social drinking acceptable."

—BOB JONES III
Chancellor, Bob Jones University, Greenville, South Carolina

"Dr. Jaeggli has presented a compelling case as to why Christians should abstain from the consumption of alcoholic beverages. If you are a believer who is seriously committed to proper biblical interpretation and application, you will be instructed, challenged, and encouraged by reading this treatise."

—STEVE PETTIT
President, Bob Jones University, Greenville, South Carolina

"Dr. Jaeggli gives us the benefit of diligent research and careful exegesis of Scripture. This book is a great addition to this important discussion. It verifies in careful detail what I believe is a proper conclusion upon a first reading of the Scriptures that bear upon this subject—the Bible teaches abstinence from strong drink."

—KEITH WIEBE
Senior Pastor, Grace Gospel Church, Huntington, West Virginia
President, American Association of Christian Schools, East Ridge, Tennessee
President, West Virginia Christian Education Association

"*Christians and Alcohol: A Scriptural Case for Abstinence* is a must-read. I wish I had read this book early in my ministry before preaching incorrect information in a sincere effort to discourage drinking. Dr. Jaeggli's scholarship is thorough, his arguments well-reasoned, his writing clear and concise. Dr. Jaeggli 'hope[s] the reader will carefully consider the validity of [his] methodology and conclusions and be persuaded in his own mind concerning what he should believe about this important subject.' Surely, the objective reader will conclude, along with Dr. Jaeggli, and many others of us, that total abstinence is the only position to take."

—JOHN VAUGHN, DPASTH
President, Fundamental Baptist Fellowship International
Senior Pastor (retired), Faith Baptist Church, Taylors, South Carolina

"Randy Jaeggli's inductive investigation of the question of whether Christians are at liberty to drink alcoholic beverages will prove to be a valued resource for pastors and laymen alike. It is marked by careful workmanship with texts, their words and contexts, ancient backgrounds and customs as well as relevant contemporary considerations. Engaging illustrations illuminate the discussions. All of this is presented with simplicity, remarkable brevity, and refreshingly unambiguous and unapologetic applications. I'm grateful to have this tool available."

—MARK MINNICK, PHD
Senior Pastor, Mount Calvary Baptist Church, Greenville, SC

"With his early background in aspects of chemical engineering and then many years of teaching Hebrew and Old Testament courses, Dr. Jaeggli has just the right skills for handling this highly pertinent topic of the Christian and alcohol. With careful exegesis, fascinating explanations of chemical processes, and well-reasoned and firm conclusions, Dr. Jaeggli provides an invaluable resource and clear guidance in these days of undiscerning Christianity."

—ALAN PATTERSON, PhD
Administrative Director, GFA Missions, Greenville, South Carolina

"Randy Jaeggli's *Christians and Alcohol: A Scriptural Case for Abstinence* is written not just to be understood, but to not be misunderstood. Leaving no stone unturned in research while repeatedly sounding clear warnings, this book is an outstanding read for those with a heart to really know and do what the Bible teaches regarding drinking. Since some sincere believers at times unwittingly embrace inaccurate information in their zeal for a particular cause, Jaeggli carefully exposes and kindly dismantles the myths used by well-meaning souls to forward the teetotalers' cause. Instead he uses the weight of biblical truth illustrated by eye-opening historical fact to demolish Satan's lies about the 'moderate' use of wine in modern times and presents a compelling case for total abstinence. If you've ever wondered whether social drinking is legitimate in our day, and you have a heart to obey God, this book will be used by the Spirit to convince you to shun all use of alcohol as a beverage."

—JOHN R. VAN GELDEREN, DPasTh
Evangelist and President, Revival Focus Ministries, Forest City, North Carolina

"This is a refreshingly thorough biblical exegesis and historical analysis, coming together with a passionate, spiritually reasoned application for the twenty-first-century believer."

—JOSEPH HELM JR., JD
Associate Pastor, Brookside Baptist Church, Brookfield, Wisconsin
Attorney, McLario, Helm & Bertling, Menomenee Falls, Wisconsin

"Dr. Jaeggli is to be commended for his rigorous contextual exegesis, his careful theological analysis, and his insightful practical application. Every Christian who desires to honor the Lord on this issue would greatly benefit from this work. The author's methodology should also serve as a model of applied theology on other disputed questions of Christian ethics."

—DAVID SHUMATE, PhD, JD
General Director, MGM International, Phoenix, Arizona

CHRISTIANS AND ALCOHOL
A SCRIPTURAL CASE FOR ABSTINENCE

RANDY JAEGGLI

BOB JONES
UNIVERSITY PRESS
Greenville, South Carolina

Library of Congress Cataloging-in-Publication Data

Jaeggli, Randy, 1952- author.
  Christians and alcohol : a scriptural case for abstinence / Randy Jaeggli.
    pages cm
  Includes bibliographical references.
  Summary: "Considers objectively the crucial question of whether Christians today should be drinking alcoholic beverages even in moderation, thoroughly examines the clear biblical evidence from both the Old Testament and the New Testament as well as historical factors, and confidently affirms that total abstinence in the scriptural choice"--Provided by publisher.
  ISBN 978-1-60682-489-4 (perfect bound pbk. : alk. paper) 1. Temperance (Virtue)
2. Drinking of alcoholic beverages. 3. Temperance--Biblical teaching. I. Title.
  BV4647.T4J345 2014
  241'.681--dc23
                                    2013047296

BWHEBB, BWHEBL, BWTRANSSH [Hebrew]; BWGRKL, BWGRKN, and BWGRKI [Greek] Postscript® Type I and TrueType T fonts Copyright © 1994–2006 BibleWorks, LLC. All rights reserved. These biblical Greek and Hebrew fonts are used with permission and are from BibleWorks, software for biblical exegesis and research.

Unless otherwise noted, all Scripture quotations are from the King James Version. Scripture quotations marked NASB are taken from the New American Standard Bible®, Copyright © 1960, 1962, 1963, 1968, 1971, 1972, 1973, 1975, 1977, 1995 by The Lockman Foundation (www .Lockman.org). Used by permission. Scripture quotations marked NIV are taken from the Holy Bible, New International Version®, NIV®. Copyright © 1973, 1978, 1984, 2011 by Biblica, Inc.™ Used by permission of Zondervan (www.zondervan.com). All rights reserved worldwide. "NIV" and "New International Version" are trademarks registered in the United States Patent and Trademark Office by Biblica, Inc.™

The fact that materials produced by other publishers are referred to in this volume does not constitute an endorsement of the content or theological position of materials produced by such publishers.

Christians and Alcohol: A Scriptural Case for Abstinence
Randy Jaeggli

Design and page layout by Michael Boone

To John F. Mitchell,
my esteemed father-in-law,
who made the decision as a young adult
to repudiate alcoholic beverages
and set an excellent example for his children.
I admire him greatly for his loving leadership
and warm reception of me into his family
over thirty-three years ago.

CONTENTS

Preface

Drinking alcohol is the single greatest substance-abuse epidemic in American society. Governmental statistics annually reveal that a shocking percentage of major crimes committed in the United States such as assault, rape, and murder are fueled by alcohol. Billions of dollars is lost each year due to damaged health, work absenteeism, and automobile accidents caused by alcohol abuse.

Regularly the *Chronicle of Higher Education,* an esteemed publication for those engaged in college teaching and administration, reports with clinical accuracy and carefully supported research the rising plague of constant alcohol abuse and chronic binge drinking by students on college and university campuses across America. Even the calmest assessments present the facts as a monstrous problem.

To these disturbing assessments may be added the fact that the business, professional, social, and recreational spheres of life in America are infused with the casual and constant consumption of intoxicating alcoholic beverages. It is a normal part of virtually all social occasions of any kind, from casual evenings out to well-planned parties, from christenings to weddings, from birthdays to anniversaries, from promotions to retirements, from Christmas parties to funerals. Drinking alcohol is, in fact, a cultural expectation—if not a requirement—for the sophisticated American adult.

The discerning Christian can confidently assert that drinking alcohol to the point of impairment or even serious intoxication is a normal and accepted sin of "the world," to use biblical language that describes those who follow current cultural mores. The "world's" behavior naturally follows since most in America, though nominally Christian, relegate God and the Christian morality taught in the Bible to a relatively peripheral part of their concern or experience.

What should be alarming to the Christian is not that the world acts like the world with alcohol, but that the church has begun acting like it. Recent surveys of evangelical college students show that well over 90% see no problem with the consumption of alcohol socially, while thirty years ago similar surveys revealed that virtually all evangelical and fundamental college students believed total abstinence from alcohol consumption was the right practice for a Bible-believing Christian.

Today, students from even the most conservative, biblically-focused Christian colleges are "rethinking" their view of drinking. They wonder, "Does Scripture really forbid drinking alcohol? There seem to be positive statements about it in the Bible. Even Christ turned water into wine at the wedding feast of Cana. Isn't drinking alcohol permissible according to Scripture as long as it is done in moderation?"

In this book, *Christians and Alcohol: A Scriptural Case for Abstinence*, Randy Jaeggli of the Bob Jones University Seminary faculty answers these questions and many more. Step by step, he shows with meticulous biblical evidence, medical facts, historical discussion, and mature pastoral reasoning why the believer who is concerned about walking in purity and holiness should never drink alcohol.

Arguments in favor of drinking in moderation are refuted in this book. Claims that all the wine commended in the Bible is un- fermented grape juice are shown to be false through the careful examination of terms used for alcoholic beverages in the Bible and the accumulation of the historical, cultural, and archaeological evidence from both the Old Testament era and the first-century world of the New Testament. Most importantly, Dr. Jaeggli shows irrefutably that what was consumed by believers in the first cen- tury was not the intoxicating alcoholic beverages of today and that their practices then are no justification for any level of alcohol con- sumption today.

Perhaps the greatest contribution of this book is the deft, scholarly modeling of how careful scriptural exegesis and correct biblical in- terpretation can give clarity to a subject that at first reading the Bible seems to present in an unclear way. Dr. Jaeggli honors the God he loves and serves through this book by showing that He is the Light of the world on this topic, as He is on all others, and not the author of confusion. This book demonstrates that the Scrip- tures, the Word of God, are always sufficient to fully equip the Christian for life and service (2 Tim. 3:16–17).

Stephen J. Hankins, Dean
Seminary and Graduate School of Religion
Bob Jones University

INTRODUCTION
WHY TALKING ABOUT DRINKING MATTERS TODAY

I did not grow up in a Christian home. I first heard the gospel at the age of twelve (in 1964) while watching an evangelist on television. I had no idea that a Bible-believing church existed until some family friends invited us to one. The pastor was a gifted exegete: unfortunately, I never heard preaching that dealt with practical issues of how a believer's understanding of Scripture should affect his lifestyle—*unless the Bible stated the matter very explicitly.* I remember a series of messages on the book of Ephesians, for instance, in which the pastor took a strong stand against any form of sexual immorality (see Eph. 5:3–7) but completely glossed over the command to "have no fellowship with the unfruitful works of darkness, but rather reprove them" (Eph. 5:11). I remember when the issue of the Charismatic Movement stirred no small amount of controversy, but no one ever debated the question of whether or not Christians should drink alcoholic beverages. I suppose the people at church simply assumed that drinking was outside the realm of legitimacy for a Christian.

The Lord graciously gave me a keen appetite for reading and studying Scripture as I began my freshman year in college. The cultural environment in the early 1970s on a secular college campus was not at all conducive to Christian growth. Every day I found myself on the spiritual frontlines of battle. I needed to saturate myself with the Word and find camaraderie in spiritual warfare with a group of Christian friends. I joined an evangelical campus organization that emphasized aggressive witnessing to our fellow students.

It was not long, however, before I began to notice that my Christian friends and I had come to some different conclusions about practical issues of lifestyle. One day I was having lunch with some of these friends at a favorite campus restaurant known for its fabulous pizza. They ordered a pitcher of beer and quaffed with no apparent qualms. Then they noticed that I was not joining them in their choice of a beverage. It seemed to me that drinking on campus was a good example of the "unfruitful works of darkness" that a Christian ought to shun. I saw the disaster that alcohol was producing in the lives of unsaved students. Drunkenness was destroying their study time, fueling their sexual immorality, robbing them of their health, and sometimes even killing them in horrible car accidents. I wondered why a Christian would want to have any association with drinking. We are new creatures in Christ, I thought, not worldly people enslaved by a mind-altering substance. Scripture instructed me in holiness of lifestyle and exhorted me to manifest a zeal for being like Christ instead of modeling my life after the world system (see 1 John 2:15–17). When I tried to explain my objections to my friends, however, they called me a legalist.

Problems associated with drinking on the secular college campus have certainly not diminished since the 1970s. Drinking alcohol produces consequences every year that "are more significant, more destructive, and more costly than many Americans realize," according to a report by a task force commissioned by the National Institutes of Health (a branch of the U.S. Department of Health and Human Services), which presented the results of a three-year study.[1] Please keep in mind that the following statistics represent what happens *every year* to college students between the ages of 18 and 24 as a result of alcohol consumption on American campuses:

- 1,825 deaths from alcohol-related injuries, including car accidents
- 599,000 unintentional injuries
- 690,000 assaults by another student who has been drinking
- 97,000 sexual assaults or date rape
- 150,000 health problems

Scripture exhorts believers, "The night is far spent, the day is at hand: let us therefore cast off the works of darkness, and let us put on the armour of light. Let us walk honestly, as in the day; not in rioting and drunkenness . . . . But put ye on the Lord Jesus Christ, and make not provision for the flesh, to fulfil the lusts thereof" (Rom. 13:12–14). If no other passage in the Bible addressed the idea of staying as far away as possible from enslaving desires and living like a child of God with a clear-cut testimony of salvation, this one would be enough to convince me to avoid the consumption of alcohol.

Since my college days I have seen an increasing number of believers decide that the issue of drinking is a matter of personal preference within what they perceive as a "gray area" of Christian liberty. Indeed, attitudes toward drinking have been changing in evangelicalism for more than fifty years. Even though throughout the first half of the twentieth century most Bible-believing Americans held

---

[1]"College Drinking," National Institute on Alcohol Abuse and Alcoholism, accessed October 7, 2013, niaaa.nih.gov/alcohol-health/special-populations-co-occurring-disorders /college-drinking [statistics based on R. Hingson, W. Zha, and E. Weitzman, "Magnitude of and Trends in Alcohol-Related Mortality and Morbidity among U.S. College Students Ages 18–24, 1998–2005," *Journal of Studies on Alcohol and Drugs* 16 (July 2009): 12–20].

to a position of abstinence, attitudes toward drinking began to change in the 1960s. James Davison Hunter analyzed a survey of what students from nine evangelical liberal-arts colleges and seven evangelical seminaries believed concerning a wide range of theological and moral issues. The largest change in students' views concerning standards of moral conduct involved the issue of drinking alcoholic beverages. In 1951, 98% of students in these evangelical institutions agreed that it was always wrong to drink alcohol, but that percentage dropped to only 17% in just over three decades.[2]

These statistics are remarkable. Any thinking person should wonder how such a global shift in Christian thinking could possibly have taken place. Perhaps the primary cause is the development of a pervasive skepticism concerning authority that has developed in our culture since the 1960s. People have become much less likely to accept a particular standard simply because someone in spiritual authority over them asserts it to be true and proper. In our cultural milieu many people care little about what older people say or what conventional wisdom has long maintained as true. Probably an errant philosophy of Christian living that rejects specific application of the doctrine of separation from the world system has also taken its toll.[3]

The purpose of this book is to examine the issue as objectively as possible. Regardless of how this global shift in thinking has come about, those who imbibe alcoholic beverages today include sincere

---

[2]James Davison Hunter, *Evangelicalism: The Coming Generation* (Chicago: University of Chicago Press, 1987), 58–60.

[3]Some contemporary Christians have misunderstood the Bible's teaching on Christian liberty. They insist that it is legalistic to apply biblical principles to issues of Christian conduct not enunciated explicitly in Scripture. They have rejected the idea that the biblical doctrine of sanctification mandates a circumspect life of personal holiness. For a refutation of this distorted view of sanctification, see my book *Love, Liberty, and Christian Conscience* (Greenville, SC: Bob Jones University Press, 2007).

believers who want to walk with the Lord and please Him. There
have also been some capable biblical interpreters who have concluded
that drinking in moderation is within the realm of permissible conduct for the Christian. To say that the question about drinking has
become highly controversial is an understatement for sure.

The purpose of this book is to examine the issue as objectively as
possible. The reader has probably concluded (correctly) from this
short introduction that I have personally adopted a position of
total abstinence from alcohol as a beverage. The reader may also
have concluded (incorrectly, I hope) that I am, therefore, inca-
pable of handling the issue objectively. Please do not be quick to
make that assumption!

My goal is to evaluate the question of drinking from an exegetical methodology. Exegesis is the objective process of drawing out
from a scriptural text the meaning that the Holy Spirit intended.
The admonition of 2 Corinthians 4:2, that the Bible interpreter
must not be guilty of "walking in craftiness, nor handling the
word of God deceitfully,"[4] demands application of Scripture that
rests securely on sound exegesis—not the interpreter's imagination
or what he would like Scripture to say. I hope the reader will carefully consider the validity of my methodology and conclusions and

---

[4]Philip E. Hughes observes that "while Paul speaks of the purity and candour of his
ministerial conduct, it is evident from the whole context of this epistle that he does so
not out of concern for his own reputation, but rather that by implication he is con-
trasting himself with others whose behaviour has been inconsistent with their claims
to be ministers of Christ." *Paul's Second Epistle to the Corinthians*, New International
Commentary on the New Testament, ed. F. F. Bruce (Grand Rapids: Wm. B. Eerdmans
Publishing Co., 1962), 122. The Greek word translated *handling deceitfully* is δολοω,
to "falsify" or "adulterate." W. F. Arndt and F. W. Gingrich, *A Greek-English Lexicon of
the New Testament and Other Early Christian Literature* (Chicago: University of Chicago
Press, 1957), 202. These crafty preachers were guilty of the "wresting of passages from
their context and their misapplication" (ibid., 123).

be persuaded in his own mind concerning what he should believe about this important subject.

GRAMMATICAL INTERPRETATION

The process of accurately expressing the meaning of Scripture entails several key components.[5] Lexicography, the study of word meaning, is of vital importance. Biblical usage determines meaning. The interpreter also studies the grammatical relationships between words in particular verses. Analysis of word meaning and grammar yields the objective meaning the Holy Spirit intended His Word to convey. In the following pages the reader will find an analysis of the way Scripture uses various Hebrew and Greek words for *wine* and *strong drink*.

HISTORICAL INTERPRETATION

We must be very careful, however, what we conclude from the study of word meaning and grammar. Were the alcoholic beverages that people consumed in the biblical period equivalent to what people drink today? Historical analysis is the second key component of proper interpretation, and it is absolutely crucial in the issue of wine usage. Why did people in ancient days drink alcoholic beverages? Were these beverages the equivalent counterparts of modern wine and beer, or were they diluted significantly before consumption? Are there historical disconnects between drinking in the ancient setting and drinking today? The answers we give to these questions are an essential component of correct biblical interpretation—they are not simply peripheral issues. I intend to show that ancient people significantly diluted their wine.

---

[5]The discussion that follows describes the exegetical process in a general overview, but readers who desire a more in-depth description may want to read Walter C. Kaiser Jr., *Toward an Exegetical Theology: Biblical Exegesis for Preaching and Teaching* (Grand Rapids: Baker Book House, 1981). My overview loosely follows Kaiser's presentation.

Beverages produced from grains instead of grapes, drinks that our English translations typically call *strong drink* or *beer*, may have had a concentration of ethanol as low as 0.5%. People in biblical days sometimes lacked sources of potable water that would not make them ill. Certainly some people in ancient days drank because they wanted to become drunk, just as some do today. Paul found it necessary, for instance, to denounce certain wealthy people in Corinth who were coming to the Lord's Supper in a drunken state (1 Cor. 11:20–22)! But generally most people today drink much more intoxicating alcoholic beverages for different reasons, resulting in highly significant cultural differences between drinking in biblical days and drinking today.

CONTEXTUAL INTERPRETATION

Careful study of the context of a passage of Scripture is the third aspect of Bible study. If an interpreter does not do justice to context, his interpretative conclusions may be erroneous. I have a favorite illustration I like to use with students in order to reinforce this truth. Fred is a new believer and has no idea how to study his Bible. A friend at church suggests that every morning Fred should take his Bible, close his eyes, open the text to a random page, place his finger on a random verse, open his eyes, and read his verse for the day. The first time Fred tries this method he lands on Matthew 27:5, which says, "And he cast down the pieces of silver in the temple, and departed, and went and hanged himself." Unable to discover the blessing in this verse, Fred tries the method again and lands on a verse that says, "Then said Jesus unto him, Go, and do thou likewise" (Luke 10:37). Putting the two verses together, Fred is quite puzzled and a bit alarmed! Still hopeful, Fred gives the method one last try. This time he reads, "Then said Jesus unto him, That thou doest, do quickly" (John 13:27). Three strikes and you're out! Now Fred is convinced the Bible teaches the doctrine of rapid suicide! By taking verses out of context we could be guilty of crafting a doctrine that is entirely foreign to the true teaching of the Bible.

There is nothing wrong, *per se*, with building doctrinal truth by assembling verses from a wide range of passages, as long as one does not violate the contextual meaning of the verses. The Bible interpreter must also keep in mind that there are various levels of context, all the way from the paragraph in which the verse appears to the overall teaching of the entire Bible on a particular subject. So when we are examining verses that relate to the issue of drinking, we cannot simply pick out a few of our favorites that support our position and ignore a whole class of verses that do not.

THEOLOGICAL INTERPRETATION

The final aspect of careful Bible interpretation is theological analysis, which involves both biblical theology and systematic theology. Though there are some important differences between the two, they are both valid and essential. Biblical theology emphasizes inductive analysis—starting with the biblical data, looking for the function and inter-relatedness of the data, and deriving general conclusions. It is also sensitive to the chronological development of biblical revelation as God progressively develops a subject throughout the history of the writing of Scripture. As a biblical theologian, I have approached the study of drinking from this inductive perspective, moving from specific information to general conclusions. Systematic theology enters the picture as a framework for an understanding of how the issue of drinking relates to the great doctrines of the Bible. We must always make ethical decisions in relation to how the gospel impacts the believer's life. As Christians we must be striving for personal holiness by applying truths about Christ to the way we live daily. We must take our sanctification seriously, instead of seeing how closely we can model the world system that is passing away.

> *A sound interpretative analysis of the biblical data mandates that Christians today refrain from alcoholic beverages.*

So what does the Bible say? And how are we to apply what it says to the issue of drinking today? There is an apparent paradox in how drinking is presented in the Bible. Scripture sometimes states that wine is a blessing to God's people (e.g., Ps. 104:15) and other times calls it a horrible curse (e.g., Prov. 23:29–35). Historically, some have explained this seeming paradox by maintaining that the "wine" the Bible mentions as a blessing is really grape juice. This is not the conclusion I have reached. I hope to persuade readers that a sound interpretive analysis of the biblical data, together with an understanding of the crucial importance of being good stewards of our bodies, mandates that Christians today wisely refrain from any consumption of alcoholic beverages.

1

Four Crucial Considerations on the Drinking Issue

The perspective we have is often crucial in understanding life's issues. Our outlook on even relatively unimportant considerations can determine whether or not we understand what is happening. A few years ago, when photos from satellites became available, I was fascinated by the views I could get of the properties our hunting club leases in Union County, South Carolina. One of our enterprising club members wandered around the woods with his GPS unit, visited all our hunting stand locations, and then plotted them on printouts of these satellite maps. Because logging roads and ATV trails rarely go in straight lines, I was surprised to learn from a bird's eye view that some stands were actually much closer together than I had ever imagined. One should not underestimate the value of a macroscopic perspective (the "big picture"), especially on important ethical issues. Before we analyze specific scriptural information on the question of drinking, let's examine some crucial considerations that should control our thinking on the subject.

Crucial Consideration #1:
Fermentation of Grape Juice Was Unavoidable

We must be careful not to read back into the Scripture our modern knowledge of microbiology. We can make a trip to the grocery store and purchase grape juice, a product of the modern process of pasteurization (unknown before the 1860s). But ancient people did not have the knowledge of microorganisms that we have, and they did not possess the technologies of sterilization and hermetic sealing that are common in our day.

Ancient people would harvest their grapes, place them in the upper section of a wine vat, and stomp them with their bare feet. Wine vats were often hewn into solid rock. They did not use a high-pressure press (as they did with olives) because they did not want to crush the grape seeds and make the wine bitter. Juice flowed from the upper section to a lower collection basin (or series of basins), where it would begin to ferment almost immediately in the open air.[1] This first stage of the fermentation process produced such significant amounts of carbon dioxide gas that the juice appeared to be boiling.

After four to seven days of rapid fermentation, workers would draw the wine out of the vat and pour it into pottery jars or wine-skins for the second stage of the fermentation process to proceed to completion. Fermentation continued until one of two conditions terminated the process: (1) the yeast exhausted the supply of sugar in the juice, or (2) the level of ethanol in the wine reached the point of fatal toxicity for the yeast. This second phase of fermentation lasted between two and four months before the wine would be ready for consumption.[2] It was important for the ancient producer to exclude as much air as he could during this second phase because bacteria could utilize the oxygen to produce acetic acid (vinegar) from the ethanol—thus souring the wine.

---

[1]Barry L. Bandstra notes that "in the warm climate of Palestine fermentation began almost immediately after the grapes were pressed. The first stage of fermentation took place in the winevat." "Wine Press, Winevat," *International Standard Bible Encyclopedia* (Grand Rapids: William B. Eerdmans Publishing Company, 1988), 4:1072.

[2]A. C. Schultz, "Wine and Strong Drink," *Zondervan Pictorial Encyclopedia of the Bible*, ed. Merrill C. Tenney (Grand Rapids: Zondervan Publishing House, 1976), 5:938.

Today we can keep grape juice from fermenting, and it is delicious and completely non-intoxicating. The fact that people in Scripture drank wine during a time when it was impossible to keep grape juice from fermenting does not give people today license to drink.

Crucial Consideration #2:
MODERN ALCOHOLIC BEVERAGES ARE FAR MORE INTOXICATING

The next big idea for our consideration involves the historical reality that modern alcoholic beverages are far more intoxicating than the diluted wine that ancient people typically drank. Because grape juice started fermenting so quickly after the grapes were crushed, drinking unfermented grape juice was possible only during grape harvest (in August and September in Palestine). Of course undiluted wine was available for people in the ancient world to drink if they wanted to get drunk, but such a practice did not meet with societal approval. In drinking undiluted wine, people in Bible times violated the warning of Proverbs 23:31, "Look not thou upon the wine when it is red, when it giveth his colour in the cup, when it moveth itself aright."[3] Trying to compare modern drinks with the *diluted* wine that people in ancient days commonly consumed is like the proverbial attempt at comparing apples and oranges. It is illegitimate to justify the consumption of modern wine simply by observing that even godly people drank diluted wine in biblical times.

Dilution of wine in Jewish culture

The practice of diluting wine with water in the ancient world is so well attested in historical sources that it is *undeniable*. We will begin our historical focus in Old Testament times by considering statements we find in the Talmud. I realize that there are very

---

[3]For a full analysis of this key verse, see Chapter 2 (pp. 53–57).

few Christians who have spent much time reading this interesting source of information on Jewish life and interpretation, so a brief description is in order. The Talmud was written between AD 100 and 500. It contains two main divisions, the Hebrew Mishnah and the Aramaic Gemara. The Mishnah "contained a digest of all the oral laws (supposedly communicated by word of mouth from Moses to the seventy elders), traditions, and explanations of Scripture."[4] The Mishnah presents these traditions in six orders: agriculture, feasts, women, civil and criminal law, sacrifices, and unclean things. These orders are further divided into sixty-three tractates. The Gemara contains a more detailed commentary on various aspects of the Mishnah. The Talmud is important to the study of drinking practices because it is a window into the lives of God's chosen people, showing specific details of how they lived. The traditions the Talmud describes extend well back into Old Testament times, and modern Jewish people revere Talmudic statements nearly to the same degree as the Scriptures themselves.

Michal Dayagi-Mendels, Frieder Burda Curator of Israelite and Persian Archaeology at the Israel Museum in Jerusalem, notes that

> the technique of mixing wine was a discipline of its own. The Talmud relates that the sage Rava excelled at this task, and his mixed wines were renowned far and wide (BT Bava Metzia 60a). In general, the wine was mixed in a ratio of two-thirds wine to one-third water, or two-thirds water to one-third wine (Mishnah Niddah 2:7). There were also

---

[4]Gleason L. Archer Jr., *A Survey of Old Testament Introduction, Revised and Expanded* (Chicago: Moody Publishers, 1994), 70.

other ratios, but the rule of thumb was to observe the local custom.[5]

During the Hellenistic through the Roman-Byzantine period, "it is known that the Jews, like the ancient Greeks and Romans, avoided strong, concentrated wine, which the Talmud calls *yăyĭn hai* ["living wine"]; instead they drank only wine that had been mixed with water. This was not only to avoid becoming intoxicated, but also because diluted wine was healthier than plain water, which was known to be contaminated."[6] Clearly Dayagi-Mendels is describing a significant historical difference between the diluted beverages that ancient Israelites drank for health reasons and the alcoholic drinks people consume today. Robert H. Stein asserts, "In ancient times there were not many beverages that were safe to drink. . . . The safest and easiest method of making the water safe to drink, however, was to mix it with wine."[7] People in biblical times wanted to drink water that would not make them sick; they generally wanted to avoid intoxication (of course, there were exceptions); they liked the taste of diluted wine because ancient wine was often strongly flavored; and they wanted to make their expensive wine go further by diluting it.

Stein cites the Talmudic tractate Shabbath *77a*, which specified a dilution ratio of two parts water to one part wine.[8] Tractate Pesahim 108*b* directed the one who drank his four cups of wine for the Passover celebration to dilute the wine in a 3:1 ratio. Various

---

[5]Michal Dayagi-Mendels, *Drink and Be Merry: Wine and Beer in Ancient Times* (Jerusalem: The Israel Museum, 1999), 60. Dayagi-Mendels presents the objective viewpoint of an archaeologist on the issue of drinking in the ancient world.

[6]Ibid.

[7]Robert H. Stein, "Wine Drinking in New Testament Times," *Christianity Today,* June 20, 1975, 10.

[8]Ibid.

rabbis argued with one other about what the optimal dilution ratio ought to be.[9] Although the ratio of water to wine was variable, the virtually universal practice of dilution is undeniable. See Table 1 for selected quotations from the Talmud concerning dilution of wine with water.

TABLE 1. SELECTED QUOTATIONS ABOUT THE DILUTION OF WINE IN JEWISH CULTURE

Source	Quotation
Michael L. Rodkinson, trans., "Tract Sabbath," *New Edition of the Babylonian Talmud*, 2nd ed. (Boston: New Talmud Publishing Company, 1903), 1:143–44.	"The prescribed quantities (of victuals and beverages) prohibited to be carried about on the Sabbath (are as follows): Sufficient wine in a goblet, which with the addition of a certain quantity of water would make a full goblet of wine (fit to drink). . . . Wine which is not strong enough to be mixed with three parts of water is not considered wine at all."
Michael L. Rodkinson, trans., "Tract Pesachim," *New Edition of the Babylonian Talmud* (Boston: New Talmud Publishing Company, 1899), 5:210, 226.	"On the eve of any Passover it is not lawful for a person to eat anything from the time of Min'hah (afternoon prayer) until after dusk . . . Nor shall a person have less than four cups of wine. . . . R. Jehudah said in the name of Samuel: 'Each cup must contain wine which, when mixed with three parts of water, will be good wine.'"

In addition to these Talmudic statements, the apocryphal book of 2 Maccabees indicates that the Jews diluted their wine with water during the intertestamental period of Israel's history. "For as it is hurtful to drink wine, or water alone; and as wine mingled with water is pleasant, and delighteth the taste: even so speech finely

---

[9]Michael L. Rodkinson, *New Edition of the Babylonian Talmud*, 2nd ed. (Boston: New Talmud Publishing Company, 1903), 1:143.

framed, delighteth the ears of them that read the story" (2 Macc. 15:39).[10]

Dilution of wine in Greco-Roman culture

The Greeks and Romans, like the Jews, sought to reduce the likelihood of drunkenness by diluting their wine. Maynard Amerine notes another reason for cutting wine with water: "The wine of classical antiquity, however, was very different from modern wine. Both Greeks and Romans lined storage vessels with resin [to keep them from leaking], which imbued the wine with its taste. They often flavored their wine heavily with spices, herbs, flowers, and perfume, and always diluted it with water before consumption, probably to dilute the strong flavoring. *Only barbarians drank undiluted wine.*"[11] Dayagi-Mendels maintains that "the Greeks did not drink wine at mealtimes, but mainly at banquets (symposia) held after the meal. They used to mix their wine with water in different ratios, such as 3:2 or 3:1, which enabled them to drink large quantities at a time. *The drinking of undiluted wine was considered barbaric*; it was, as the Greeks put it, 'to drink like a Scythian.' Herodotus writes that King Cleomenes of Sparta, under Scythian influence, adopted the custom of drinking undiluted wine and went mad as a result."[12] At the Greek symposium, "the host decided on the ratio of water to wine to be employed and on the pace of the drinking for that evening. The ratio was generally determined on the basis of the type of wine being served and on its strength. The traditional proportions were 3:1, 5:2, or 5:3; in

---

[10] *The Holy Bible: 1611 Edition, King James Version* (Nashville: Thomas Nelson Publishers, 1982). I have modernized the spelling. The original King James Version included the Apocrypha between the Old Testament and the New Testament.

[11] Maynard A. Amerine, "Wine," *Collier's Encyclopedia*, ed. Lauren S. Bahr (New York: P. F. Collier, 1996), 23:518 (emphasis added).

[12] Dayagi-Mendels, 71.

certain instances, the wine was so strong that it had to be mixed at a ratio of 20:1. The resulting alcohol content of the drink *was less than what is common for modern-day beer*."[13] See Table 2 for selected quotations concerning dilution of wine in Greco-Roman culture.

TABLE 2. QUOTATIONS ABOUT THE DILUTION OF WINE
          IN GRECO-ROMAN CULTURE

Source	Quotation
Plutarch's Moralia in Sixteen Volumes, Frank Cole Babbitt, trans. (Cambridge, MA: Harvard University Press, 1971), 2:265–67, 403.	"For wine is the most beneficial of beverages, the pleasantest of medicines, and the least cloying of appetizing things, provided that there is a happy combination of it with the occasion as well as with water. Water, not only the water that is mixed with the wine, but that which is drunk by itself in the interim between the draughts of the mixture, makes the mixture more innocent."
	"Achilles told Patroclus to strengthen the mixture because he knew that older men like Phoenix and Odysseus prefer their wine strong rather than watery."
Plutarch's Moralia in Sixteen Volumes, Paul A. Clement and Herbert B. Hoffleit, trans. (Cambridge, MA: Harvard University Press, 1969), 8:267–69.	"'Five,' indeed, is in the ratio 3:2, three parts of water being mixed with two parts of wine; 'three' is in the ratio 2:1, two parts of water being mixed with one of wine; and four,—three parts of water being poured into one of wine. . . . The mixture with ratio 2:1 brings on that disturbing and half-drunk pitch of intoxication."

---

[13] Dayagi-Mendels, 88 (emphasis added).

Source	Quotation
Pliny: Natural History in Ten Volumes, H. Rackham, trans., in The Loeb Classical Library, ed. E. H. Warmington (Cambridge, MA: Harvard University Press, 1968), 4:221–23, Book 14.6.54.	"Homer has recorded the mixing of Maronean wine with water in the proportion of 20 parts of water to one of wine. This class of wine in the same district still retains its strength and its insuperable vigour, inasmuch as one of the most recent authors, Mucianus, who was three times consul, ascertained when actually visiting that region that it is the custom to mix with one pint of this wine eight pints of water."
Athanaeus, *The Deipnosophists*, Charles Burton Gulick, trans., in Loeb Classical Library, ed. T. E. Page (Cambridge, MA: Harvard University Press, 1961), 4:431, Book 10.426c.	"Then Democritus said: 'Hesiod, my comrades, advises us to pour forth thrice of the water, and to put in the fourth part of wine'. . . . For they say one should drink two parts wine to five of water, or one part wine to three of water."

Ancient people had to be very careful about the water they drank because some sources might be contaminated by surface run-off and airborne pathogens. Drinking water from the typical well (the Hebrew word is *be'er*) might make people ill. There were artesian springs (the Hebrew word is *'ayin*)[14] that produced safe drinking water, and population centers grew up around these precious sources of potable water. When Abraham's servant arrived at the city of Nahor, for example, Rebekah gave him a drink from the spring *('ayin*, Gen. 24:16) and asserted that she would water his thirsty camels. The camels, however, were given water from the well (*be'er*, 24:20). Just as in many places in the world today, people in biblical times sought safe alternatives to tainted water. The modern situation in countries like ours with water treatment

---

[14]On the contrast between the well (*be'er*) and the spring (*'ayin*), see Jean-Georges Heintz, "בְּאֵר," in *Theological Dictionary of the Old Testament*, ed. G. Johannes Botterweck and Helmer Ringgren, trans. John T. Willis (Grand Rapids: William B. Eerdmans Publishing Company, 1977), 1:463.

systems is far different. We have numerous sources of safe hydration, so the underlying motivation for the consumption of alcoholic beverages in our day is at odds with the reasons for drinking diluted wine during the biblical period.

Historical analysis is a key interpretational tool for an expositor of Scripture. The Lord has providentially made available to us numerous historical sources and archaeological discoveries that shed light on the culture, customs, and dramatic historical events of biblical days. Today's interpreter must bridge the cultural gap that exists between the time when the inspired authors of Scripture wrote and today's vastly different setting. We are better interpreters of God's Word as our knowledge of the ancient world increases through the study of historical and archaeological sources.

Wrong conclusions about drinking today

Some people today argue that Christians are free to drink alcoholic beverages because Jesus and the apostles drank. In the light of our examination of the historical differences between the biblical and modern periods, however, this argument clearly rests on *the faulty premise of equivalence between ancient and modern wine.* In order to justify the legitimacy of their position, modern proponents of drinking in moderation must deny the existence of a cultural disconnect. Kenneth L. Gentry Jr., for example, maintains that there is no evidence people in Old Testament times diluted their wine.[15] Gentry becomes strangely silent about asserting anything concerning the practice in New Testament days, a time when the secular literature on drinking practices in Greek and Roman culture abounds with detailed description of the practice of the dilution of wine with water before consumption. Before I refute Gentry's

---

[15]Kenneth L. Gentry, *God Gave Wine: What the Bible Says About Alcohol* (Lincoln, CA: Oakdown, 2001), 143–46.

view, I would like first to commend his overall exegesis and logical development in much of what he writes. But when he comes to the crucial point of examining the issue of dilution, his argumentation is incomplete and misleading. Although Gentry himself does not drink alcohol due to a medical problem that precludes it, he thinks it is proper for Christians to drink today's wine—as long as they stop short of drunkenness.

Gentry asserts that the Scriptures are silent about any practice of the dilution of wine with water in Old Testament times.[16] Even if Gentry's assertion were right (which, as we shall see, it is not), arguments from silence are never very strong. The burden of proof that people in the Bible commonly drank undiluted wine (contrary to the practice of their cultural setting) is a severe difficulty that falls on proponents of drinking in moderation. Gentry does not consider Talmudic statements about the dilution of wine. His assertion that the Old Testament is silent on the issue of dilution of wine with water fails to consider Proverbs 9:2. Solomon tells us in this verse that wisdom personified "hath killed her beasts; she hath mingled her wine; she hath also furnished her table." The Hebrew word translated *mingled* is a verb that simply means "to mix."[17] It occurs only five times in the Old Testament, including its use in Proverbs 9:2. In Psalm 102:10 (v. 9, English), David laments that he has "eaten ashes like bread, and mingled [his] drink with weeping." Most modern translations render "with weeping" as "with tears" since the tears are produced by the action of weeping

---

[16]"First, *all* the evidence supporting this contention [that wine was diluted with water before drinking] comes from extra-biblical sources such as Pliny's *Natural History*." Ibid., 143.

[17]See William L. Holladay, *A Concise Hebrew and Aramaic Lexicon of the Old Testament* (Grand Rapids: William B. Eerdmans Publishing Company, 1971), s.v. מָסַךְ, 203. Oddly, Holladay adds in parentheses "(honey and spices)" to his definition of "mix." None of the five uses of the word mentions anything about honey or spices.

(an example of synecdoche, in which the action of weeping stands for the product of the weeping). So the psalmist's tears (consisting mostly of water) are mixed with his "drink" (a general word for a beverage). The verb "to mix" occurs in Proverbs 9:5 synonymously with its use in 9:2. In Isaiah 5:22 the prophet pronounces woe to those who are heroes in mixing "strong drink" (translated as *beer* by some modern translations). The prophet does not tell us what is being mixed into the strong drink, but the negative context of the verse suggests that it was something that enhanced the intoxicating effect of the beverage. Finally, the verb appears in Isaiah 19:14, where the Lord mixes a "perverse spirit" into the midst of the Egyptians. So an examination of the direct object of the verb "to mix" shows that sometimes the element that is mixed into something is left unspecified and other times is specified as *tears* or a *perverse spirit*.

This leaves the question open as to what wisdom personified is mixing with the wine she offers to the naive person in Proverbs 9:2. The translators of the Septuagint, the Greek translation of the Hebrew text completed about 150 BC, help us in answering this question. They chose an interesting rendering of the Hebrew verb "to mix" in 9:2, reflecting the common practice of diluting wine with water. They translated the verb as "to mix in a bowl" (ἐκέρασεν εἰς κρατῆρα). The Greek word for "bowl" (κρατήρ, *krater*) appears often in secular Greek literature in referring to a large mixing bowl used for combining wine with water before consumption. Stein notes that in ancient times wine was stored in large jugs called *amphorae*. When people wanted to drink it, they poured wine from the *amphorae* into large mixing bowls called *kraters*, and then into cups (*kylix*).[18] From the standpoint of the

---

[18]Stein, 9.

Septuagint translators, wisdom personified mixed wine with water. Because the Septuagint was the version of the Old Testament that most people in the time of Christ read, its translation of Proverbs 9:2 is highly significant.

In addition to denying that Old Testament people diluted their wine as a common practice, Gentry also asserts that the one time the Old Testament explicitly mentions wine that has been diluted with water, it is in a negative context.[19] The verse at issue is Isaiah 1:22, which says, "Thy silver is become dross, thy wine mixed with water." In context this verse describes one aspect of the deplorable conditions that existed in Judah. Jerusalem had degenerated into a city of spiritually (and probably physically) adulterous people. Instead of being inhabited by the righteous, now it was full of murderers (1:21). The rulers were companions of thieves, and bribery was rampant. Justice was being trampled in the court system (1:23). Sandwiched between 1:21 and 1:23, the statement about impure silver and adulterated "wine" must, indeed, be negative.

We should start our investigation of the verse by noting that the word translated *wine* occurs only here and two other places in the Old Testament (Hos. 4:18; Nah. 1:10), compared to 141 occurrences of the most common term translated *wine*. The Hebrew noun is *sobe'* (סֹבֶא) and is related to the verb meaning "carouse, drink hard." Holladay uses the generic word *drink* to translate *sobe'* and speculates that it may have been a type of beer made from wheat.[20] In fact, the *Holman Christian Standard Bible* translates it as *beer*. Verse 22 describes Jerusalem in metaphoric terms of once-valuable commodities that have become worthless. Jerusalem is

---

[19]Gentry, 145.
[20]Holladay, s.v. סֹבֶא, 251.

pictured as beautiful silver that has become dross (lead oxide),[21] the byproduct of the refining process of lead-silver ore. Similarly, Jerusalem is a once-valuable drink that has been adulterated by contamination from some unknown source of water and is now unfit to drink. It is also possible that the *sobe'* has been diluted with water by an unscrupulous merchant, so that he is cheating his customer by selling an adulterated product. This is a far different scenario from a customary dilution of wine with water before consumption. Because Gentry rejects the idea that people in Bible times diluted their wine before drinking it, he concludes that it is fine for Christians today to drink the 12–14% ethanol wine available on the market. Such a conclusion is erroneous and dangerous.

Crucial Consideration #3:
SCRIPTURE WARNS ABOUT THE DANGER OF ALCOHOL

Our third crucial consideration involves the strong warnings the Bible contains about the use of alcoholic beverages. Someone might object to the use of verses that warn of alcohol *abuse* as a reason for staying away from alcohol entirely. But we must emphasize that even the moderate use of alcohol can lead to addiction and abuse. I find Daniel Akin's perspective on this point very helpful: "Moderation is not the cure for the liquor problem. Moderation is the cause of the liquor problem. Becoming an alcoholic does not begin with the last drink, it always begins with the first. Just leave it alone."[22] Norman L. Geisler likewise asserts that "total abstinence is the safer policy. A person cannot abuse drinking if he

---

[21]See Holladay, s.v. סֹבֶא, 255.

[22]Daniel L. Akin, "The Emerging Church and Ethical Choices: the Corinthian Matrix," in *Evangelicals Engaging Emergent: A Discussion of the Emergent Church Movement*, ed. William D. Henard and Adam W. Greenway (Nashville: B&H Publishing Group, 2009), 278.

does not drink."[23] In light of the very real possibility of addiction to alcohol through the pathway of even moderate consumption, here is an important observation: if the Bible warns us about the dangers of even the diluted alcoholic beverages of the ancient period, *these warnings are much stronger for us today in relation to the more intoxicating beverages available.* The impact of the following verses should cause us to stay away from any alcoholic beverage consumption. I quote them without any interpretive comments.

Proverbs 20:1

"Wine is a mocker, strong drink is raging: and whosoever is deceived thereby is not wise."

Proverbs 23:29–35

"Who hath woe? who hath sorrow? who hath contentions? who hath babbling? who hath wounds without cause? who hath redness of eyes? They that tarry long at the wine; they that go to seek mixed wine. Look not thou upon the wine when it is red, when it giveth his colour in the cup, when it moveth itself aright. At the last it biteth like a serpent, and stingeth like an adder. Thine eyes shall behold strange women, and thine heart shall utter perverse things. Yea, thou shalt be as he that lieth down in the midst of the sea, or as he that lieth upon the top of a mast. They have stricken me, shalt thou say, and I was not sick; they have beaten me, and I felt it not; when shall I awake? I will seek it yet again."

---

[23]Norman L. Geisler, "A Christian Perspective on Wine-Drinking," *Bibliotheca Sacra* 139 (January–March, 1982): 54.

Isaiah 5:22

"Woe to them that are mighty to drink wine, and men of strength to mingle strong drink."

Isaiah 28:7–8

"But they also have erred through wine, and through strong drink are out of the way; the priest and the prophet have erred through strong drink, they are swallowed up of wine, they are out of the way through strong drink; they err in vision, they stumble in judgment. For all tables are full of vomit and filthiness, so that there is no place clean."

1 Corinthians 6:9–10

"Know ye not that the unrighteous shall not inherit the kingdom of God? Be not deceived: neither fornicators, nor idolaters, nor adulterers, nor effeminate, nor abusers of themselves with mankind, nor thieves, nor covetous, nor drunkards, nor revilers, nor extortioners, shall inherit the kingdom of God."

Crucial Consideration #4:
CHRISTIAN LIBERTY HAS LIMITS

I believe the scriptural warnings above ought to settle the issue of drinking. But perhaps some will still insist that drinking falls within the sphere of matters that the Bible does not settle explicitly. So for a moment I will argue as if I agreed (though I do not) with the premise that the question of drinking today exists within a "gray area" of Christian liberty. Our fourth big idea is this: Christian liberty has limits, and the consumption of today's alcoholic beverages is outside the boundaries of acceptable behavior for the believer.[24] Here are three principles from 1 Corinthians 6:10–13 that demonstrate this big idea.

- **Christians should avoid anything that is inherently prone to enslave them.**

Those who are determining their position on whether or not they will drink alcoholic beverages must take into account certain physiological and genetic issues. Most sin does not physically alter a person's brain and is unrelated to his genetic makeup. Consider, for instance, the sin of lying. There is no known permanent alteration of brain function occurring through a pathway of biochemical mechanisms when a person says something that he knows to be untrue. There is no genetic propensity for lying (except that we are all descended from Adam!). We must never excuse drunkenness as due simply to genetic propensity or biochemical alteration of brain function as if people bear no responsibility for their drinking. Alcoholism is a sin. The alcoholic made wrong choices that led to his enslavement to alcohol. He chose to drink excessively and to rebel against the warnings of Scripture. But this slavery was facilitated by alcohol's effect on the brain in creating long-lasting, intense memories of the euphoric experience. There is also a genetic propensity to alcoholism, especially in families where alcohol abuse has already surfaced as a problem.[25] These two considerations make drinking the highly alcoholic beverages of our day a potentially

---

[24]For similar argumentation, see Akin, 262–80.

[25]I discuss these biochemical and genetic considerations in Chapter 5. Gentry attempts to deflect the impact of biochemical considerations when he asserts, "The notion that alcoholism is somehow a physiological defect is antithetical to the biblical doctrine of sin and of personal responsibility" (131). I would maintain, however, that the doctrine of sin and an awareness of the genetic propensity that some people manifest toward alcoholism together inform a full view of the potential enslavement that alcohol may produce. I do not minimize the sinfulness of alcoholism by recognizing the existence of biochemical pathways that lead to addiction. Rather, I observe how especially dangerous it is to drink alcohol.

addictive activity. Even secular sources admit that alcohol is the most widely abused modern drug, far surpassing the devastating effects of illicit drugs such as heroin, cocaine, and methamphetamines. The United States Center for Disease Control, the most respected source on the devastating effects of alcohol, informs us that "alcohol is used by more young people in the United States than tobacco or illicit drugs. Excessive alcohol consumption is associated with approximately 75,000 deaths per year. Alcohol is a factor in approximately 41% of all deaths from motor vehicle crashes."[26] Enslavement to alcohol truly produces massively destructive consequences. It is a vicious, cruel taskmaster.

Today's believer must follow Paul's example: "All things are lawful unto me, but all things are not expedient: all things are lawful for me, but I will not be brought under the power of any" (1 Cor. 6:12). The translators of some modern versions put quotation marks in 6:12 around the phrase, "Everything is permissible for me," in order to imply that this was an assertion the Corinthians were making, but that Paul is arguing against. Thiselton asserts that "there can be no question that the initial clause of v. 12 represents a quotation used as a maxim by some or by many at Corinth."[27] These Corinthian believers had developed an unbalanced view of Pauline teaching concerning the believer's freedom from the demands of the Mosaic law. They supposed that Christian liberty

---

[26]"Alcohol and Drug Use," Centers for Disease Control, accessed September 2, 2009, http://www.cdc.gov/healthyYouth/alcoholdrug/index.htm.

[27]Anthony C. Thiselton, *The First Epistle to the Corinthians: A Commentary on the Greek Text*, New International Greek Testament Commentary, ed. I. Howard Marshall and Donald A. Hagner (Grand Rapids: William B. Eerdmans Publishing Company, 2000), 460. Ben Witherington III agrees that the phrase "everything is permissible for me" is a Corinthian slogan, and he lists additional ones that Paul quotes later in the epistle: "It is good for a man not to touch a woman" (7:1); "All of us possess knowledge" (8:1); "No idol in the world really exists" (8:4); "Food will not bring us close to God" (8:8); and "There is no resurrection of the dead" (15:12). *Conflict and Community in Corinth* (Grand Rapids: William B. Eerdmans Publishing Company, 1995), 167.

gave them the right to do whatever they wanted rather than the liberty to manifest a lifestyle commensurate with their union with Christ. The context following 6:12 shows the nearly incredible extent to which the Corinthians were applying their errant view of liberty: they thought it was all right for a Christian to employ the services of a prostitute (6:13–20). They had become so enslaved to their appetite for sexual relations that they were willing to go outside the parameters of God's will in order to fulfill their lust.

The next phrase in 6:12, "be brought under the power," translates the Greek verb *exousiasthēsomai* (ἐξουσιασθήσομαι), "to be mastered."[28] Paul was wary of anything that might enslave him. First Corinthians 6:12 follows an extensive list that describes the sinful lifestyles of those who are headed for perdition. The drunkard, included in this list of sinners, has no ground for assurance of salvation (6:10). Surely no one who claims to know Christ as Savior would willingly want to place himself in a position of potential enslavement to alcohol.

The timeless general principle of avoiding anything with the potential for enslavement rings down through the ages of church history with a clarion tone. Certainly it is possible to abuse just about anything. I really enjoy good food, for instance. As I eat a meal, I am aware that when I reach the point of satiety, I should stop eating. If I am not careful, I could cross over the line of propriety and become a glutton. Instead of eating to live, I could love food so much that I live to eat. But I am willing to risk possible addiction to food because I have to eat in order to survive. My continued survival does not depend, however, on my consumption of alcoholic beverages. There is, therefore, no legitimate comparison in

---

[28]See Arndt and Gingrich, 278.

modern America between avoiding the sin of gluttony and avoiding drunkenness. When I become thirsty all I have to do is place a glass under the kitchen faucet, turn on the tap, and slake my thirst with pure, safe water. If I tire of the monotony of drinking only water, other options include iced tea, fruit juice, sports drinks, or soda. I have absolutely no reason to drink an alcoholic beverage and put myself at risk for becoming enslaved. There is a sure-fire method for never becoming an alcoholic: do not drink any alcoholic beverages even in moderation. This simple action of abstinence is in full accord with the Pauline principle of avoiding enslavement. Akin astutely observes, "True spiritual freedom is not the right to do what you want; it is the supernatural enablement of Christ to do what you ought and enjoy doing so!"[29]

• Christians should embrace only what edifies.

We have many options for how we spend our time and money. Through the internet we have access to an entire world of information about anything our inquisitive minds might desire. We are all aware that cyberspace contains both helpful and extremely harmful content. We need to be able to differentiate not only between what is good and bad, but also between what is good, better, and superior. In the same verse that Paul expressed his resolve to avoid anything that might enslave him, he also affirms that not everything was *expedient* for him (1 Cor. 6:12). The Greek word translated *expedient* is the verb *sumpherei* (συμφέρει), meaning "to help, confer a benefit, be advantageous or profitable or useful."[30] Many things we might choose to do are not necessarily wrong, but they offer no positive benefit toward building us up in our relationship with Christ. Time is a very precious commodity. Our lives go by

[29]Akin, 267.
[30]Arndt and Gingrich, 787.

quickly, just as a person's breath appears for a brief time on a cold winter's morning and then vanishes in an instant (James 4:14). We should invest our time wisely.

If we should avoid activities that lack spiritual profit, how much more then should we repudiate actions that might ruin us and others? Every believer has influence over someone else's life. We must examine our lives carefully to make sure we are not leading someone astray by our example. It can happen easily. Parents are especially aware of how their children imitate everything they do. When our oldest son was about two years old, we bought him a little toy lawnmower because he seemed so interested in watching me whenever I mowed the grass. Just after he got the toy mower, I noticed the next time I was out mowing that he was following me with his new toy. Everywhere I went, he followed. Suddenly the magnitude of the responsibility of being a parent became even clearer to me. I realized anew that it was my responsibility to pray for my children, to teach them the Scripture, to bring them to a Bible-preaching church, to provide them with a loving example of what our gracious Savior is like, and to establish godly standards in daily living. I needed to steer them toward what would build them up in faith in Christ.

My wife and I agreed that alcoholic beverages were completely antithetical to the goals we had set for our children's edification. What possible profit could the use of alcohol have in our home? We wanted to teach our children the importance of separation from the world system, not how to become camouflaged Christians that blend into a worldly lifestyle undetected. Believers must not manifest the same ungodly lifestyle of those they are seeking to evangelize.

All believers, regardless of whether or not they are parents, must likewise realize that someone is watching their lives with the intent of imitating them. Junior high teens scrutinize what older high school young people do. Newly married couples like to get together with couples who have been married a little while longer in order to acquire tips for developing a successful marriage. Singles who have just graduated from college watch the lives of other singles who have been living successfully on their own. Believers who have just been saved pay close attention to the lifestyle of those who are more mature in the faith. Nearly everyone has at least some influence on someone else. We must use that influence to edify others for their spiritual profit. Drinking alcoholic beverages does absolutely nothing to edify anyone.

• Christians should act only from a motivation of love.

Edification flows from a motivation of love for Christ and fellow believers. Living in light of the gospel means that I respond daily in my lifestyle choices to the great love that Christ demonstrated when He willingly gave His life on the cross to pay the penalty for my sins. The Christian life is not grim duty or grudging obedience to a set of rules. It is rather a joyful response of faithfulness and obedience to the one who loved me and gave Himself for me. By virtue of His sacrifice for me, Christ literally bought the entirety of my being, and now I am no longer my own. "What? know ye not that your body is the temple of the Holy Ghost which is in you, which ye have of God, and ye are not your own? For ye are bought with a price: therefore glorify God in your body, and in your spirit, which are God's" (1 Cor. 6:19–20). When a person comes to faith in Christ, he should no longer live on the basis of what he wishes to do or what seems right from his human understanding—but rather from a motivation of love for the Savior who bought him.

Paul placed love above faith and hope (1 Cor. 13:13). He asserted that astounding verbal ability means nothing without love (13:1). Having love is superior to understanding even the greatest mysteries and being able to communicate what will happen in the future (13:2). The most astounding acts of philanthropy would profit nothing without it (13:3). Love bears anything and knows no limit of humility (13:4). It always produces generosity of spirit (13:5). Love and truth are inseparable companions (13:6). Love endures anything life can throw at it (13:7).

Love sacrifices anything personal for the benefit of other people. A loving person is able to forego an activity that would not be problematic for him but that might produce ruin in someone else's life. This is the main idea of Paul's instruction to the Corinthians concerning whether or not to eat meat that might have been sacrificed to idols. Although Paul clearly states that participation in any kind of meal in the venue of an idol temple is wrong (1 Cor. 10:20–21), perhaps there would be other opportunities to eat meat when its origin was unknown. Paul enunciated the principle that a loving concern for other people should govern a believer's conduct in such situations: "Let no man seek his own, but every man another's wealth" (10:24). If an unbeliever invites a Christian to dinner and serves meat, the believer should feel free to eat it— as long as no one identifies it as meat that has been sacrificed to an idol. Paul asserts that he lives to "please all men in all things, not seeking mine own profit, but the profit of many, that they may be saved" (10:33).

The believer who walks in love is very careful not to put a stumbling block in the way of another person: "But take heed lest by any means this liberty of yours become a stumblingblock to them that are weak" (8:9). In Paul's day the Greek word for a stumbling block (*proskomma*) referred to a rough road that was difficult to traverse. Figuratively it conveyed the idea of an obstacle to a person's plans or chosen lifestyle.[31] In the context of 1 Corinthians 8:9, the "weak" person could be tempted to fall back into the idolatry from which he claimed to be saved. The "stumblingblock" is, therefore, a serious matter and not something that simply annoys another person. It causes real spiritual impediment. If a believer is not careful to live in loving concern for the spiritual lives of others around him, then he is living sinfully: "Through thy knowledge shall the weak brother perish, for whom Christ died? But when ye sin so against the brethren, and wound their weak conscience, ye sin against Christ. Wherefore, if meat make my brother to offend, I will eat no flesh while the world standeth, lest I make my brother to offend" (8:13).

Of course, the issue of eating food sacrificed to idols has ceased to be a concern for us. But there are still issues today that require a loving caution for the possible effect certain actions might have on other people. Consider the following scenario: You meet a new family at church one Sunday and invite them to your house for a snack after the evening service. You have no idea that before the husband was saved, he was an alcoholic. He battled with his addiction for months after he came to Christ but finally understood enough of the Bible to walk in victory over his former enslavement. What would happen to someone like this if you were to offer him a glass of wine or a bottle of beer with his meal? Would you want to be the precipitating cause of his falling back into alcohol abuse? What if he simply saw alcoholic beverages in your refrigerator and assumed that if you, a mature Christian, could drink, then so could he? Would that be a loving thing to do?

---

[31]Ibid., 723.

A person who walks in love manifests wisdom, the ability to anticipate the consequences his actions might have on other people. If I love my children, for example, I will raise them in a home that promotes only wholesome influences. If I love my coworkers in my secular workplace, I will show them the testimony of a Christian who loves Christ—not the world system. If I love my fellow church members, I will seek to build them up in devotion to Christ. Consumption of alcoholic beverages is incompatible with all these responsibilities.

CONCLUSION

We ought to take Paul's instruction in Romans 14 to heart. It is uncertain what exact problem Paul was facing with these believers at Rome. Perhaps the person who was "weak in the faith" (Rom. 14:1) was a believer with a Jewish background. Although he was not trusting in his adherence to the Mosaic law as the ground of his salvation (as the Judaizers in the book of Galatians were), he still considered dietary restrictions and holy day observances as vitally important aspects of his Christian life.[32] It is also possible that those who were weak in faith were Gentiles who believed that a lifestyle of self-denial was incumbent on a Christian. Whatever the case, Paul commands the other Christians at Rome to treat the weak person with sanctified deference. They should be careful in their conduct "not to put an obstacle or a stumbling block" in his way (14:13, NASB) because that would be a completely unloving thing to do (14:14–15). Here Paul adds to the word *obstacle* (*proskomma*)

---

[32]Douglas J. Moo concludes that "the 'weak' were Jewish Christians (and probably also some Gentile 'god-fearers') who believed that they were still bound by certain 'ritual' requirements of the Mosaic law." *The Epistle to the Romans*, New International Commentary on the New Testament, ed. Gordon D. Fee (Grand Rapids: William B. Eerdmans Publishing Company, 1996), 831. See also Thomas R. Schreiner, *Romans*, Baker Exegetical Commentary on the New Testament, ed. Moisés Silva (Grand Rapids: Baker Academic, 1998), 707, 730.

an even stronger Greek word for something that is a trap or an enticement to sin (*skandalon*).[33] Believers ought to be willing to forego eating or drinking anything that would produce ruin in the life of another because "the kingdom of God is not meat and drink; but righteousness, and peace, and joy in the Holy Ghost" (14:17). In fact, "it is good neither to eat flesh, nor to drink wine, nor any thing whereby thy brother stumbleth, or is offended, or is made weak" (14:21). I do not know anyone who would suffer shipwreck of his faith if he saw me eating meat, but I can surely envision the deleterious effects that might result if I were to take a permissive stand on drinking alcohol—even in moderation. Someday I am going to give account of myself to God (14:12). I must, therefore, live in such a way that no one experiences spiritual disaster or physical ruin as a result of my example.[34]

---

[33]See Arndt and Gingrich, 760.

[34]As Moo correctly observes, "The believer who seeks the peace and edification of the church should gladly refrain from activities that might cause a fellow believer to suffer spiritual harm" (861).

2

WHAT PEOPLE IN OLD TESTAMENT DAYS WERE DRINKING

Now that we have these crucial considerations in mind, the next step in examining the issue of drinking is to look at the specific information the Bible presents on the topic of what people in Old Testament days were really drinking. Scripture is completely sufficient for a mature Christian life of service for God that is based on sound doctrine (2 Tim. 3:16–17). Our task is to make sure we do a good job of interpreting the Bible, lest we formulate our standards for Christian living on a faulty understanding of what God has actually revealed to us.[1] Our discussion focuses on the words the Old Testament uses in referring to fermented liquids, translated in our English versions as *wine* and *strong drink* (or *beer*). Because all natural beverages from fruit and grains were fermented and not distilled, none of them had an alcohol content of more than 14%.[2] It is likely that most ancient wine was nowhere near that 14% level, due to the production of grapes with lower sugar content than modern vintages and the far less controlled conditions of the fermentation process than exist in

---

[1] Careful exegesis is the essential foundation for all application of Scripture. The discussion that follows necessarily involves some technical details of Hebrew word meaning and usage.

[2] Nonfortified wines range from 8% to 14% ethanol. The percentage of sugar in the grape at the time of harvest (most wine grapes contain 21-25% sugar) and the specific kind of yeast involved in fermentation determine the final percentage. Fermentation ceases at around 14%, no matter how high the sugar content of the grape juice, because that concentration of ethanol is lethal to the yeast. See Amerine, 23:517–21.

modern winemaking.[3] On top of that, as we saw in Chapter 1, people in Bible days diluted this lower-alcohol wine with water, producing a beverage that was non-intoxicating unless consumed in huge quantities.[4] Distillation can produce a much higher ethanol content but was not discovered until the Middle Ages. Ancient people knew nothing of alcoholic drinks as strong as the whiskey produced in more modern times up to the present.

The production of wine was a lot of work. Isaiah 5:1–7 describes God's relationship with Judah in the language of viticulture. First, the Lord looked for a spot to plant His vineyard until He found the perfect "fruitful hill." He then dug up the soil, cleared away the rocks, and planted the best type of vine. He built a watchtower in the vineyard to protect it from human thieves or destructive animals. The last step was to hew a wine vat out of solid rock. After all that work, the Lord earnestly expected a good vintage. But instead of good grapes, the Lord's vineyard produced sour ones. Isaiah 5:1–7 does not use any of the biblical words for beverages that result from stomping grapes, but the passage does show that wine was the result of considerable enterprise. The Old Testament uses several words to describe the product of the vineyard.

---

[3]Concerning the lower alcoholic content of ancient wines, Andre S. Bustanoby observes, "I am convinced that one reason why alcohol abuse was not a major problem to the ancients is that truly good, high-alcohol wine was not in great supply and was thus expensive. There was a lot of poor-quality wine of low-alcohol content. And a lot of it never became true wine—it was just aerobically fermented must." *The Wrath of Grapes: Drinking and the Church Divided* (Grand Rapids: Baker Book House, 1987), 30.

[4]"There is evidence that relatively large quantities of fermented wine could be drunk because it was liberally diluted with water. This was a custom among the Jews in Old Testament times as well as among the Greeks and Romans in the first century. *Wine drinking in those days was more a challenge to the bladder than to the equilibrium.*" Ibid., 25 (emphasis added).

YĂYĬN

The most common word in the Old Testament for a beverage with alcoholic content is *yăyĭn* (יַיִן pronounced *yah´·yin*), translated by the English word *wine*. This Hebrew word occurs 141 times, so a careful study of each usage in its context is a time-consuming task. For those with limited time, several standard sources are available.[5] (See Appendix 1 for a list of all the uses of *yăyĭn* in their contextual setting. This table contains the results of an inductive analysis of the Hebrew word, something that anyone can do using Bible study software.) In any word study, the most important thing to keep in mind is that the actual usage of the word in the Old Testament determines its meaning.

After a thorough analysis of the uses of the Hebrew word, the interpreter can begin to sort these uses into groups that convey similar ideas. Sometimes *yăyĭn* appears in favorable contexts with other agricultural items that sustain people's lives. Other uses indicate a substance that people can easily abuse, and drunkenness is the result. Since drunkenness is such a deplorable state, *yăyĭn* is an appropriate metaphor for picturing the horrible effects of God's judgment. As a substance with such potential for producing disaster, sometimes *yăyĭn* occurs in contexts that completely prohibit its use.

---

[5]See W. Dommershausen, "יַיִן," in *Theological Dictionary of the Old Testament*, ed. G. Johannes Botterweck and Helmer Ringgren, trans. David E. Green (Grand Rapids: William B. Eerdmans Publishing Company, 1990), 6:59–64; Eugene Carpenter, "יַיִן," in *New International Dictionary of Old Testament Theology and Exegesis*, ed. Willem A. VanGemeren (Grand Rapids: Zondervan Publishing House, 1997), 2:439–41; and R. Laird Harris, "יַיִן," in *Theological Wordbook of the Old Testament*, ed. R. Laird Harris (Chicago: Moody Press, 1980), 2:375–76.

Wine as a Blessing

A safe, flavorful source of hydration was a blessing to people in ancient Palestine. They did not have dozens of different beverages from which to choose, as we do. Although there were springs that were famous for supplying life-sustaining water (for example, Gen. 16:7), and there were also some wells from which people could drink safely (for example, 2 Sam. 23:14–17), other wells could be polluted by surface run-off and were fit only for watering livestock (Gen. 24:13–20). Just like today in many places in the world, tainted water produces illness even in people whose immune systems are generally able to handle relatively high levels of nasty microorganisms.

An essential part of biblical interpretation is an avoidance of reading our cultural setting back into the Old Testament. Next to the regular faucet on my kitchen sink, for instance, is a smaller tap that dispenses water from my reverse osmosis filtration system. Before the water even enters the reverse osmosis filter, it goes through an activated charcoal pre-filter. Before it goes to the tap, the water passes through another charcoal finishing filter. One cannot imagine purer water anywhere on earth, except for distilled water. All I have to do is flip a lever and I have all the safe water I need. Our municipal system never runs dry. Dying of thirst has never even crossed my mind. Obtaining an adequate supply of fluids, however, was a constant concern for ancient people. This concern was greatest during hot summer months, especially when a person was exerting himself physically.

The wrong way to explain how wine can be a blessing

Some authors who correctly promote the position of abstinence from alcohol incorrectly maintain that when the Bible says something good about *yăyĭn*, it must be unfermented grape juice.

Robert P. Teachout, a scholarly advocate of this view, states that "this same Hebrew word [*yăyĭn*] can legitimately refer to two distinctly different grape beverages. The first would be *unfermented juice* and the second would be fermented, *intoxicating wine*" (emphasis original).[6] Teachout admits that his view is held by very few people in conservative circles, but he is undeterred by the unpopularity of his position.[7]

In a review article of Teachout's work, J. A. Witmer astutely concludes that "though Teachout provides much helpful material, it appears that his position stated above is essentially a presupposition imposed on the evidence rather than a conclusion validly drawn from it."[8] It is vitally important that we undertake our interpretive investigations with objectivity and let the Scripture dictate what we believe, rather than approaching the Bible with a presupposition in mind that our investigation will by all means support.

We have seen already that grape juice begins to ferment almost immediately after grapes are stomped in the wine vat. Yeast naturally resides on the surface of the grapes, and there is no way to keep this yeast from entering the juice as the treading process occurs. Even though fermentation started rapidly, the Hebrews did have a word for unfermented juice, and this word is *mishrah*. It appears only once in the Old Testament (Num. 6:3), a fact that is commensurate with the brief amount of time it took for juice to begin fermentation. After all, if the juice existed for only a few hours per year, one would not expect to find a lot of references in the Bible to its consumption. Numbers 6:3 says concerning the

---

[6]Robert P. Teachout, *Wine, The Biblical Imperative: Total Abstinence* (n.p.: 1983), 15.
[7]Ibid.
[8]J. A. Witmer, "Review of Robert P. Teachout, *Wine, The Biblical Imperative: Total Abstinence*," *Bibliotheca Sacra* 141 (October–December, 1984): 368.

person who took the vow of a Nazirite, "He shall abstain from wine and strong drink; he shall drink no vinegar, whether made from wine or strong drink, neither shall he drink any *grape juice* [lit. "*mishrah* of grapes"], nor eat fresh or dried grapes" (NASB). This verse is important because it describes the wide spectrum of beverages made from the grape or other agricultural sources. The Nazirite was, first of all, to abstain from *yăyĭn* ("wine"), grape juice that had gone through initial rapid fermentation and then slower fermentation to the point of the completion of the process. The second drink that was forbidden to the Nazirite was *šĕkār* ("strong drink"). Our later discussion will demonstrate that this was a fermented beverage made from grain or possibly other fruits besides grapes. "Vinegar" is the product of bacterial oxidation of ethanol to acetic acid and resulted from poor control of the fermentative process. The Nazirite vow not only precluded the consumption of any alcohol, but it also put unfermented *mishrah* of grapes on the list of banned items. In the progression of terms, the Nazirite was also denied the non-beverage items of fresh grapes or raisins.

Brown, Driver, and Briggs state that the noun *mishrah* means "juice" and is related to the verb *sharah* (meaning II). The cognate verb is used in Arabic with the meaning "to be moist." In Late Hebrew the verb means "to soften or dissolve." There is an Aramaic cognate meaning "grape juice."[9] Holladay agrees that *mishrah* means "grape juice or grape extract" when it appears in Numbers 6:3 with the Hebrew noun for "grape."[10] The important point we must not miss is this: the Old Testament writers had a word for unfermented grape juice, but they used it only once! If these writers had wanted to describe unfermented grape juice,

---

[9]Francis Brown, S. R. Driver, and Charles A. Briggs, *Hebrew and English Lexicon of the Old Testament* (Oxford: Oxford University Press, 1975), s.v. "שׁרה" and "מִשְׁרָה," 1056.

[10]Holladay, s.v. "מִשְׁרָה," 222.

they had an uncontested word for it in their verbal repertoire. They used the word *yăyĭn* 141 times, sometimes in contexts where drunkenness occurred—so obviously it could be fermented. There is *no* compelling explanation for why the biblical authors did not use *mishrah* if they wanted to describe unfermented grape juice without any misunderstanding. Nevertheless, Teachout insists that *yăyĭn* is a general word, sometimes used of both fermented and unfermented grape products. He maintains that there are usages of the word that demand the meaning of "grape juice."

Teachout interprets *yăyĭn* as a reference to grape juice in Genesis 49:11. This verse is a part of Jacob's blessing on Judah: "He washed his garments in *yăyĭn*, and his clothes in the blood of grapes." Teachout views *yăyĭn* as synonymous with "the blood of grapes," which he says is grape juice. But are the two items actually synonymous? Victor P. Hamilton correctly maintains that they are different things: "It is clear that *wine* is not exactly the same as *grapes' blood*. The first refers to the finished product. The second refers to the crushing of the grapes."[11] That we are dealing with figurative language in this verse is apparent from the fact that people do not launder their clothing in wine or grape juice. Hamilton maintains that the metaphor of washing clothes in *yăyĭn* refers to God's blessing on Judah, whereas the picture of the blood of grapes is a terror of impending judgment on those who reject God.[12] Isaiah later draws on this imagery of the one who treads a winepress and stains His garments with the blood of His enemies (Isa. 63:1–3).

---

[11]Victor P. Hamilton, *The Book of Genesis, Chapters 18–50*, New International Commentary on the Old Testament, ed. R K. Harrison and Robert L. Hubbard (Grand Rapids: William B. Eerdmans Publishing Company, 1995), 662.

[12]Ibid.

Another category of verses presents *yăyĭn* as a product of a wine-press. Grape juice *is* expelled from the grape in a winepress, but this is *not* proof that *yăyĭn* must mean grape juice in certain cases. In Isaiah 16:10, for example, the prophet tells us, "Gladness is taken away, and joy out of the plentiful field; and in the vine-yards there shall be no singing, neither shall there be shouting: the treaders shall tread out no *yăyĭn* in their presses; I have made their vintage shouting to cease." There are two Hebrew words that English versions usually render as "wine vat" or "winepress." The first word is *gath*, the flat, upper portion of the winepress where workers stomped the grapes.[13] The biblical authors use this word in contexts where they want to emphasize the immediate prod-uct of crushing the grapes (for example, in Isa. 63:2). The second word is *yeqeb*, the lower vat into which the grape juice flowed and began the process of fermentation.[14] Isaiah uses the word *yeqeb* in 16:10. It was in the *yeqeb* that initial fermentation began almost immediately. Not until after this rapid fermentation was complete was the wine drawn off for the second, slower stage of fermenta-tion. So *yăyĭn*, not grape juice, was truly the product of the *yeqeb*. There is no Old Testament usage of *yăyĭn* that demands the inter-pretive conclusion that it was grape juice.

The correct way to explain how wine can be a blessing

The most important clue concerning why the Scripture some-times presents wine in a positive light is the use of *yăyĭn* in the Old Testament in association with items that were staples in a typical diet. *Yăyĭn* was one of many blessings that sustained life and en-hanced its enjoyment. When Abraham was returning from battle against the multinational confederacy that had taken Lot and the

---

[13]See Holladay, s.v. "גַּת," 65.
[14]Holladay, s.v. "יֶקֶב," 141.

inhabitants of Sodom captive, he met the mysterious Melchizedek, priest of the most high God. Melchizedek supplied Abraham with bread and *yăyĭn* (Gen. 14:18), just what the patriarch required to replenish his body's needs. The author of Judges tells us that the Levite and his concubine had all their needs met when they arrived in Gibeah: straw and fodder for the donkeys and bread and *yăyĭn* for themselves (Judg. 19:19). When Abigail brought David the provisions he had requested from her husband, the list of items included *yăyĭn* (1 Sam. 25:18). As David fled from Jerusalem during the rebellion led by his son Absalom, Ziba met the king with life-sustaining provisions including bread, raisins, summer fruits, and *yăyĭn* (2 Sam. 16:1–2). Ziba specifically said that the *yăyĭn* was for anyone who might be "faint in the wilderness."

Psalm 104:10–17 is perhaps the most striking passage presenting *yăyĭn* as a blessing from God for the satisfying of daily needs. God provides flowing springs of water for every wild animal of the field and bird of the heavens (104:10–12). The rain He sends causes grass to grow for cattle and food for man (104:13–14). The psalmist includes *yăyĭn* with these gifts in 104:15: "And wine that maketh glad the heart of man, and oil to make his face to shine, and bread which strengtheneth man's heart." Alexander gives a possible alternate translation of the verse: "And wine gladdens the heart of man—(so as) to make his face shine more than oil—and bread the heart of man sustains."[15] Regardless of which translation is better, it is certain that the psalmist includes *yăyĭn* in a passage that extols God for His work of sustaining life on planet earth.

---

[15]Joseph Addison Alexander, *The Psalms: Translated and Explained* (1873; repr., Grand Rapids: Baker Book House, 1975), 423–24. Alexander's translation depends on the use of the *min* preposition as comparative. The NASB takes *min* as causal:

"And wine which makes man's heart glad,
So that he may make his face glisten with oil,
And food which sustains man's heart" (Ps. 104:15).

This verse causes the reader to ponder whether wine gladdens man's heart in the sense of the alcohol's production of a somewhat euphoric state of mind, or whether the gladness is a result of recognizing that God has graciously met man's need for sustenance. The form of the Hebrew verb that means "to make something glad"[16] occurs in other contexts where something makes the human heart glad. Solomon says in Proverbs 27:9, for instance, that ointment and perfume make the heart glad. Here a glad heart finds delight in substances that please one's senses. Proverbs 15:30 says, "Light of eyes makes a heart glad" (a literal translation). The New International Version translates this verse, "A cheerful look brings joy to the heart." People like to be around others who are pleasant. Sometimes a smile and genuinely amicable greeting can lift a person's spirits. Proverbs 12:25 (NASB) states, "Anxiety in the heart of a man weighs it down, but a good word makes it glad." There is nothing like good news to brighten one's outlook on life.

Perhaps the most interesting use of the verb meaning "to make [something] glad" is found in Ecclesiastes 10:19. Here we find the elements of bread and *yăyĭn*, just as in Psalm 104:15. "For enjoyment one makes bread, and wine gladdens life, and money answers everything."[17] All three provisions a person needs in life—food, drink, and economic resources—enhance his sense of well-being and satisfaction. We may safely conclude, therefore, that Psalm 104:15 speaks of *yăyĭn* gladdening a person's heart in the sense of satisfying his personal needs and enhancing his enjoyment of life. Based on the clear meaning of this and similar contexts, *the verse does not extol the alcoholic "high" a person would get from excessive consumption of wine.*

---

[16] The verb is the *piel* of שׂמח.

[17] This is my literal translation of the verse.

The scriptural authors sometimes utilize this concept of wine as a satisfaction of life's basic needs in order to picture in metaphoric language the benefits that wisdom offers to those who come to God with receptive hearts. In Proverbs 9:2–12, Solomon personifies wisdom as someone who has set her[18] table with food and *yăyĭn*, dietary items necessary for sustaining life. Notice that 9:2 says she has "mixed her wine." Although in Chapter 1 we have already discussed this verse and the concept of diluting wine with water, we should note once again that Bruce Waltke mentions the Septuagint translators' rendering of the verb "to mix" as "to mix in a bowl." This translation reflects the ancient practice of diluting wine with water in a mixing bowl.[19]

The prophet Isaiah built on the concept of wine as one of the essential commodities for physical life as he crafted a metaphor that pictured eternal life. In the language of a vendor selling his products in the streets of Jerusalem, Isaiah cried out, "Ho, every one that thirsteth, come ye to the waters, and he that hath no money; come ye, buy, and eat; yea, come, buy wine and milk without money and without price" (Isa. 55:1). God is so gracious in

---

[18]Because the Hebrew word for *wisdom* is feminine, the English versions uniformly translate any pronouns referring to it as feminine (*she* or *her*). The reader should not think, however, that Solomon is portraying wisdom as a female. There is no masculinity or femininity implied in the gender of an inanimate noun. For a fuller discussion, see Bruce K. Waltke and M. O'Connor, *An Introduction to Biblical Hebrew Syntax* (Winona Lake, IN: Eisenbrauns, 1990), 99–110. Since Hebrew requires agreement between the gender of a noun and any verb or pronoun associated with it, the English versions may cause the reader to adopt the mistaken notion that wisdom must be symbolized by a woman.

[19]Bruce K. Waltke, *The Book of Proverbs: Chapters 1–15*, New International Commentary on the Old Testament, ed. R. K. Harrison and Robert L. Hubbard Jr. (Grand Rapids: William B. Eerdmans Publishing Company, 2004), 434. Even in light of this evidence, Waltke does not prefer the interpretation that wisdom mixes water with wine. Harris, however, maintains that "to avoid the sin of drunkenness, mingling of wine with water was practiced. This dilution was specified by the Rabbis in NT times for the wine then customary at Passover" (Harris, 2:376).

salvation that He makes eternal life free to all who will receive it.[20] Just as milk and *yăyĭn* sustain physical life, so the salvation that God offers satisfies man's soul and gladdens his heart forever.

Wine as a Curse

In stark contrast to verses that describe *yăyĭn* as a blessing, other verses describe it as a potential curse. This seeming paradox springs from the fact that overindulgence negates wine's blessing as a staple of life. People could abuse even diluted wine. Indeed fallen humans have a tragic propensity for turning good things into bad. Consider, for instance, the recreational activities many people in our society enjoy. Recreation provides good exercise and a release from the stress many of us experience. But hobbies, sports, and avid interests can often get out of control in a person's life. What started out as a good thing becomes an obsession, consuming inordinate amounts of financial resources, time, and mental planning. People in biblical times were similarly prone to take God's good gift of wine and abuse it. The biblical authors have a great deal to say about this abuse of *yăyĭn*. As we examine representative verses that warn about the destructive power of alcohol, remember that ancient people generally drank diluted *yăyĭn*. *These warnings are much stronger for us today* in a culture that knows nothing of watering down wine before consumption.

Solomon admonished his sons, "Be not among winebibbers; among riotous eaters of flesh: for the drunkard and the glutton shall come to poverty: and drowsiness shall clothe a man with rags"

---

[20]J. Alec Motyer correctly notes, "Yet alongside this emphasis on freeness, the verb *buy* is repeated. The thought of purchase is not set aside; this is no soup-kitchen, even if the clients are beggars. There is a purchase and a price, though not theirs to pay. They bring their poverty to a transaction already completed. Contextually, this is another allusion to the work of the Servant." *The Prophecy of Isaiah: An Introduction and Commentary* (Downers Grove, IL: InterVarsity Press, 1993), 453.

(Prov. 23:20–21). The word *winebibbers* translates a Hebrew participle from a verb meaning "to carouse" or "to drink hard."[21] The participle conveys the idea of habitual heavy drinking. Notice the way Solomon associates excessive drinking of *yăyĭn* with gluttony because both sins produce disastrous consequences in a person's life. Just as the glutton does not know when to push away from the table, so the alcohol abuser refuses to put his wine goblet down and walk away from his drink. Now *yăyĭn* has become a curse. Solomon declares, "He that loveth pleasure shall be a poor man: he that loveth wine and oil shall not be rich" (Prov. 21:17). Just as the "love of money is the root of all evil" (1 Tim. 6:10), so the love of pleasure is sure to produce a cursed life.

The first instance in Scripture of the sin of loving the pleasure of alcohol occurs in the account of Noah. At a time when "the wickedness of man was great in the earth" (Gen. 6:5), "Noah found grace in the eyes of the Lord" (6:8). Noah obeyed the Lord, labored faithfully in the construction of the ark, and fulfilled God's will. Through his efforts God saved the world from destruction. Sometime after Noah and his family disembarked from their floating sanctuary and God instituted a covenant with them, however, Noah planted a vineyard, drank from the wine he produced, and became drunk (Gen. 9:20–21). In his drunken state he displayed a loss of propriety by lying naked in his tent. His sin became the occasion for Ham's sin, which resulted in the curse on Canaan.[22] The reader of the Genesis narrative is absolutely astounded! After

---

[21]Holladay, s.v. סבא, 251.

[22]It is beyond the scope of our discussion to delve into what the nature of Ham's sin was or why Ham was cursed in Canaan. For an excellent discussion of Ham's sin, see Victor P. Hamilton, *The Book of Genesis: Chapters 1–17*, New International Commentary on the Old Testament, ed. R. K. Harrison and Robert L. Hubbard Jr. (Grand Rapids: William B. Eerdmans Publishing Company, 1990), 322–23. Geerhardus Vos maintains that Ham was cursed in Canaan "because he had sinned against his father, and he was punished in that particular son, because Canaan most strongly reproduced Ham's

all that God did in showing grace to Noah, this godly man could not control his intake of wine. Because this sin felled such a godly man, every believer should take warning. Noah's sin also affected succeeding generations, just as the use of alcohol commonly does today. Surely the wisest path for us is to avoid any consumption of alcoholic beverages. Why would we risk the same sort of disaster that Noah experienced?

Ingesting wine can suspend a person's sense of morality to the point where he or she will commit sexual immorality. After the deliverance of Lot from the destruction of Sodom and Gomorrah, his two daughters on sequential nights got their father drunk with wine and engaged in incestuous relations with him (Gen. 19:31–35). After both of these incestuous events, Lot was so inebriated that in neither case did he have any knowledge of when his daughter "lay down, nor when she arose" (19:33, 35). Just as in the narrative about Noah, we know that Lot was a righteous man. Abraham had received God's promise that He would not destroy Sodom and Gomorrah if ten righteous individuals lived there. Abraham successfully argued, and the Lord did not rebut his assertion, that it would be unjust for the Lord to sweep the righteous away with the wicked in judgment (Gen. 18:23–32). The angels' action of dragging Lot out of Sodom before the judgment could fall proves his righteous standing before God. The sin of Sodom tormented Lot's righteous soul (2 Pet. 2:8), but alcohol snared him and brought a curse to his entire lineage.

Consuming wine can also anesthetize a person to the extent that he is oblivious to imminent danger. In 2 Samuel 13, we encounter one of the saddest narratives in the Bible: one of David's sons,

---

sensual character." *Biblical Theology: Old and New Testaments* (Grand Rapids: William B. Eerdmans Publishing Company, 1948), 57.

Amnon, raped his half-sister Tamar. When Tamar told Absalom what had happened, he seemed to downplay the matter. But because Tamar was his full sister, Absalom's hatred of Amnon burned within his heart for two years. Finally Absalom saw his chance for revenge. He persuaded David to send Amnon and all the king's sons to a sheep-shearing event. Absalom carefully instructed his servants, "Mark ye now when Amnon's heart is merry with wine, and when I say unto you, Smite Amnon; then kill him" (2 Sam. 13:28). The phrase "merry with wine" describes a condition of inebriation.[23] The plan worked perfectly. Amnon was so drunk that he was virtually defenseless.

So it happens today that inebriated people drive their cars and are oblivious to the mortal danger that faces them down the road. People with alcohol in their bloodstreams even imagine that they are *better* drivers than when sober! We live in a technologically advanced age when our lives depend on the full use of our minds and sharp response times. In all fifty states, the legal definition of driving under the influence of alcohol is a blood alcohol content greater than 80 mg/dL (.080%). What many people do not realize, however, is that "impairment begins as low as 20 mg/dL" (.020%).[24] It is easy for a drinker to achieve a blood alcohol level of 20 mg/dL. If a person weighs between 140 and 180 pounds, all he or she has to do is consume one alcoholic drink in one hour.[25] One alcoholic drink is defined as one twelve-ounce can of beer,

---

[23]The phrase "when a heart is merry" is the Hebrew כְּטוֹב לֵב. The only other occurrence of the construction is in Esther 1:10, describing the inebriated state of King Ahasuerus.

[24]"Driving While Intoxicated: The Facts," WebMD, http://www.emedicinehealth.com/alcohol_intoxication/page7_em.htm, accessed October 17, 2013.

[25]"Driving and Alcohol," West Virginia University, Robert C. Byrd Health Science Center, http://www.hsc.wvu.edu/som/cmed/alcohol/driving.htm, accessed October 17, 2013.

one five-ounce glass of wine, or one mixed drink containing 1.5 ounces of distilled liquor.

Imagine with me the following hypothetical situation: Fred watches a football game on Saturday afternoon and consumes one twelve-ounce can of beer during the first hour of the event. Fred, who weighs 170 pounds, now has a blood alcohol level of approximately 20 mg/dL (.020%). Then his wife asks him to take a break from the game and drive to the grocery store to purchase some steak for a late-afternoon cookout. On the way to the store, a young boy rides his bicycle out of his driveway without looking to see whether traffic is coming. Fred brakes hard and desperately swerves to avoid hitting the lad, but the car strikes the bike and propels the child over fifty feet through the air. He dies on impact. The police perform a breathalyzer test on Fred and find that he is well below the legal level of intoxication. He is not charged in the accident. But the rest of his life Fred will wonder whether he might have avoided killing that child if he had been completely sober. His grief will be worsened by the realization that his response time was, in fact, degraded by his alcohol consumption. So Fred will suffer remorse for the rest of his life because he drank one can of beer. This hypothetical story is not far-fetched at all.

The strong warning of Proverbs 20:1

Consuming alcohol also destroys wisdom. Proverbs 20:1 says, "Wine is a mocker, strong drink is raging; and whosoever is deceived thereby is not wise." The *mocker* (sometimes translated *scorner* by the KJV) is the most hopeless category of fools in the book of Proverbs. If a person tries to correct a mocker, all he will get is dishonor and hatred (Prov. 9:7–8). The mocker is very proud (21:24), and the only thing to do with him is to apply corporal discipline (19:25; 21:11) or banish him (22:10). Waltke correctly notes that Solomon personifies wine in 20:1 in order to warn people that this intoxicant has the potential to produce in them the very characteristics of the mocker that he delineates throughout the book of Proverbs. "The drunkard lacks consciousness and self-control, and in dissolute madness breaks the bounds of sanctity, morality, and propriety."[26] The phrase "whosoever is deceived thereby" is literally "everyone who is staggering in it."[27] This is clearly a description of a person who is inebriated. Because wisdom is the most precious characteristic a person can possess (Prov. 8:11), a believer should view anything that causes the loss of wisdom as horrifically dangerous. Intoxicated people throw caution away, behaving immorally and recklessly. Because the alcoholic beverages in our day are so much more intoxicating than in biblical times, a Christian should never risk the loss of wisdom that drinking alcohol can produce.

The even stronger warning of Proverbs 23:31

In another passage on wisdom, Solomon issues the strongest warning to his sons about the danger of alcohol: "You should not gaze at wine when it manifests itself as red, when it gives in the cup its eye, when it walks around in a level path" (Prov. 23:31, my literal translation).

---

[26]Bruce K. Waltke, *The Book of Proverbs: Chapters 15–31*, New International Commentary on the Old Testament, ed. R. K. Harrison and Robert L. Hubbard Jr. (Grand Rapids: William B. Eerdmans Publishing Company, 2005), 126.

[27]The word translated "who is staggering" is a *qal* active participle from שׁגה. For the meaning "stagger, be unable to walk straight," see Holladay, 361. The translation of the King James Version, "whoever is deceived," incorrectly takes the *qal* participle as passive (as do some modern translations), but the KJV correctly translates the participle actively in all its other occurrences (Job 6:24; 19:4; and three times in Isa. 28:7). The *Holman Christian Standard Bible* handles the participle correctly: "Wine is a mocker, beer is a brawler, and *whoever staggers* because of them is not wise."

Solomon exposed the dangers of wine by placing a warning about the attractiveness of the beverage immediately after a description of an adulterous woman or a prostitute (Prov. 23:27–28). These immoral women are a "deep ditch" or a "narrow pit" (23:27). They lie in wait for prey, just as a robber does (23:28). Earlier in the book Solomon warned his sons that the immoral woman can make herself and her sin seem extremely attractive. "For the lips of a strange woman drop as an honeycomb, and her mouth is smoother than oil" (5:3). Here Solomon uses *lips* and *mouth* by metonymy to represent speech. The immoral woman will say anything in order to ensnare her prey. Her speech is seductive, geared to focus a man's thoughts on how desirable she is—not on her immorality. Solomon also commanded his sons not to allow the immoral woman to captivate them with her beauty (6:25). Then Solomon recounted an experience of seeing an act of seduction unfolding before his very eyes (7:6–27). The immoral woman did everything she could think of to make adultery look attractive. She told her intended victim, "I have decked my bed with coverings of tapestry, with carved works, with fine linen of Egypt. I have perfumed my bed with myrrh, aloes, and cinnamon" (7:16–17).

Solomon intended the full impact of his teaching about the immoral woman's attractiveness to inform his sons' understanding about the dangerous, pleasant appearance of wine (23:31). By centering their attention on the attractiveness of the wine, they might fall into the same sort of visually oriented trap the immoral woman sets up. Just as Solomon warned his sons to avoid any association with an immoral woman, he now applies the same strong injunction against drinking wine. The first line of 23:31 literally means, "You should not gaze at wine when it manifests itself as red." The verb that I have translated *gaze at* is *ra'ah*, normally defined "to see." This verb occurs 1,303 times in the Old Testament and often conveys much more than a simple look at something.[28] The action Solomon is forbidding his sons is a longing gaze that leads to sensory enticement. In Genesis 8:8, Noah sent out a dove *to see* whether the water had abated. His careful observation of the various activities of the dove caused him ultimately *to know* that he could exit the ark (8:11). Likewise when the Queen of Sheba came to visit Solomon, her purpose was *to see* his wisdom. Her careful observation left her astounded (1 Kings 10:4–7). Sometimes the verb *to see* means to experience the enjoyment of something. In Isaiah 44:16, for instance, the foolish idolater, who has used half a log to make a wooden idol and the other half to make a fire, says "Aha, I am warm, I have seen the fire." So when Solomon forbids his sons to "look" at wine, his prohibition involves a longing gaze that regards enjoyment of the wine as a sensory experience. Enticement always begins with the first longing gaze, so do not take it!

Just as his sons must avoid any contact with the adulterous woman, so they must also stay away from wine "when it manifests itself as red." This phrase is the translation of the Hebrew verb *'ādăm*, "to be red." The particular form of the Hebrew verb in Proverbs 23:31 is a personification of wine as showing off its red color.[29] At first it seems odd that Solomon would forbid his sons to partake of something he previously praised in Proverbs 9:2. In our discussion of that verse, however, we noted that the wine is diluted with water—but the wine in 23:31 is showing off its red color. A reasonable way to explain the strong prohibition against drinking this

---

[28]See the comprehensive article by H. F. Fuhs, "רָאָה," in *Theological Dictionary of the Old Testament*, ed. G Johannes Botterweck, Helmer Ringgren, and Heinz-Josef Fabry (Grand Rapids: William B. Eerdmans Publishing Company, 2004), 13:208–42.

[29]The verb is in the *hithpa'el* theme, and its use is estimative-declarative reflexive. See Waltke and O'Connor, 430–31 (par. 26.2f).

deeply red wine is to view it as *undiluted*. The likelihood of this interpretive conclusion is strengthened by a contrast in 23:30 with the wine that debauched people were drinking to excess: "They that tarry long at the wine; they that go to seek mixed wine." The Hebrew word translated *mixed wine* is *mĭmsāk*, literally a "mixing bowl."[30] This noun is related to the verb *mix* that we saw in 9:2. In 23:30, Solomon is describing drunkards who have to spend a long time getting drunk because they are drinking *diluted* wine, but in 23:31 he brings *undiluted* wine into the picture. This undiluted wine shows off its full red color, a sure sign to Solomon's sons that they should have none of it. Because people today drink undiluted wine, they should realize that they are recklessly violating this command.

The meaning of the next phrase, "when it gives in the cup its eye," is opaque to the modern reader. It was probably an idiom in Solomon's day. As F. J. Stendebach notes, "The eye of a metallic substance (*Hšml*) is its luster (Ezek. 1:4, 7, 27; 8:2; Dan. 10:6; etc.)." He prefers the related concept of "sparkling" in Proverbs 23:31.[31] Most modern translations render the phrase as the NASB does: "When it sparkles in the cup." This undiluted wine has a dazzling appearance.

The final phrase in Proverbs 23:31 is the most difficult of the verse: "When it walks around in a level path." The form of the Hebrew verb *to walk* in this phrase can mean "walk around," "wander," "move back and forth," "go away," or "walk (constantly)."[32] The noun for "a level path" (*mêšārîm*) has the possible nuances of "level way," "order, regulation," "justly, with justice," or "uprightness,

---

[30]See Holladay, s.v. "מִמְסָךְ," 199.
[31]F. J. Stendebach, "עַיִן," *Theological Dictionary of the Old Testament*, 11:38–39.
[32]See Holladay, s.v. "הָלַךְ," 80.

straightness, truth."[33] The translator really has a tough job figuring out what this phrase means. Most likely it was idiomatic, and we have lost the meaning of the idiom. The English versions take the context into account and translate the phrase as the NASB does: "When it goes down smoothly." Solomon is warning his sons that if they have succumbed to the appearance of the full-strength wine and have tasted some of it, they should immediately stop drinking it when they begin to sense the full alcoholic impact on their mouths and throats.

The modern equivalent of what Proverbs 23:31 prohibits happens every evening in fancy restaurants all across America. A special waiter, called a sommelier, carefully pours wine into a special glass and hands it to the patron who selected it from the menu. The patron then sniffs the bouquet, swirls the beverage in the glass, holds it up to the light, and takes a small taste. It is quite a production. The patron must be pleased with the wine's fragrance, color, overall appearance, and taste. He wants the total sensory experience an expensive wine can offer. Solomon would have been horrified if his sons had taken part in this sort of practice. But the same process of wine's seduction takes place in many other venues today. Anywhere people consume wine, whether at home or in a back alley, they put themselves in a place of great temptation. Bruce Waltke correctly observes, "At the semantic center of the saying [in 23:31] is the command not to yield to wine's temptation. Devastating consequences lampooning addiction surround [this command]."[34]

Solomon further instructed his sons that if they disregarded his warnings concerning undiluted wine, they would experience some disastrous consequences. They would discover that this wine bites

[33]See Holladay, s.v. "מֵישָׁרִים," 193.
[34]Waltke, *The Book of Proverbs: Chapters 15–31*, 262.

like a snake and stings like a viper (23:32). I like to spend time in the woods, especially during hunting season in the fall. I know there are copperheads, poisonous snakes indigenous to South Carolina, residing somewhere in the fields and forests where I walk, and I sincerely hope I never get bitten by one. If I happened to see one, there is no predicting how fast I could move away from it. Solomon viewed undiluted wine this way—as a dangerous snake to avoid with all one's energy. The next verse (23:33) warns that drunks can see some strange things[35] and say things they will regret when sober. Changing to a nautical setting, Solomon warns that a drunk is like a person who "lieth down in the midst of the sea, or as he that lieth upon the top of a mast" (23:34). In his drunken state he is so insensitive that he does not even know when someone strikes him. He is so addicted that immediately on the dawning of a new day he seeks another drink (23:35). People today ignore these warnings to their own peril.

Wine as a Metaphor of God's Judgment

Because consumption of wine can have such harmful personal consequences, it is an appropriate metaphor of God's judgment on sin. The psalmist, for example, states concerning God's dealings with His people, "Thou hast shewed thy people hard things: thou hast made us to drink the wine of astonishment" (Ps. 60:3; Hebrew, v. 5). The word translated *astonishment* occurs in the Old Testament only here and in Isaiah 51:17, 22. It refers to the staggering motion of a drunk as he attempts to walk.[36] God's judgment has severe effects and leaves people reeling from the divine anger their sin has ignited.

---

[35]The KJV translates the Hebrew as "strange women," but the feminine plural noun זָרוֹת probably means "strange, surprising things." See Holladay, 9.

[36]See Holladay, s.v. תַּרְעֵלָה, 395.

Psalm 75:8 (Hebrew, v. 9) says, "For a cup is in the hand of the Lord, and the wine foams; it is well mixed, and He pours out of this; surely all the wicked of the earth must drain and drink down its dregs" (NASB). Just as physical drunkenness produces disorientation, nausea, vomiting, and loss of the ability to protect oneself, so God's judgment produces horrific effects on those who are the recipients of it. The universality of this verse ("all the wicked of the earth") reminds the reader of the bowls of God's wrath poured out on the inhabitants of earth in the days of the Great Tribulation.[37] Revelation 16:19 announces, "The great city was divided into three parts, and the cities of the nations fell: and great Babylon came in remembrance before God, to give unto her the cup of the wine of the fierceness of his wrath." There is a certain irony in the picture of God judging people by forcing them to drink wine right to the bottom of the vessel. People have used wine in excess as part of their rebellion against Him. Now God will give them more "wine" than they care for, as they are full of His outpoured wrath.

The Old Testament prophets spoke often against drunkenness in their culture. It is no wonder, therefore, that the consequences of excessive consumption of wine should picture God's judgment on sin. For instance, God demonstrates through the object lesson of Jeremiah's linen waistband that God had rejected His completely ruined nation. As a metaphor of the judgment that was fast approaching, the Lord told Jeremiah to proclaim, "Thus saith the Lord God of Israel, Every bottle shall be filled with wine" (Jer.

---

[37]See Willem A. VanGemeren, *Psalms*, Expositor's Bible Commentary, ed. Frank E. Gaebelein (Grand Rapids: Zondervan Publishing House, 1991), 493.

13:12).[38] The thought of these storage jars[39] being full to capacity with wine was to remind the people that God was about to fill them with drunkenness and destruction (13:13). The Lord promised that He would "dash them one against another, even the fathers and the sons together" (13:14). Instead of picturing God's blessing and provision for His people, abundant wine signaled the approaching disaster of the Babylonian onslaught. Just as drunkenness produces disorientation, insensibility, and inability to recognize danger, so God's people were unaware of impending destruction.

Notable Examples of Total Abstinence

Due to the detrimental effects of wine and its well-established use as a metaphor of coming judgment, God gave us some noble examples of people who totally abstained from the fruit of the vine.

The Nazirites

Devotion to God produces sacrificial living. The earliest and most famous of the injunctions against *yăyĭn* involved the vow of the Nazirite. This was an entirely voluntary act that involved consecration of one's life totally to the Lord. The Nazirite was to abstain from any form of fermented beverage, even from nonalcoholic vinegar.[40]

---

[38]F. B. Huey suggests that this was actually a well-known proverb in Judah. "The saying may have originated as a raucous cry at a drunken feast, but it probably had become a confident expression that God would continue to prosper the people. If so, Jeremiah turned it into a promise of certain judgment. . . . 'Drunkenness' here is a figure to describe the helplessness of the people to defend themselves from the enemy's attack." *Jeremiah, Lamentations*, New American Commentary, ed. E. Roy Clendenen (Nashville: Broadman Press, 1993), 145.

[39]The Hebrew word נֵבֶל refers not to "bottles" (KJV) or "wineskins" (NIV), but to storage jars (ibid.).

[40]Fermentation is a process involving yeast that occurs in the absence of oxygen. The production of vinegar (acetic acid) is a process involving bacteria that takes place in the presence of oxygen. (Acetic acid is simply a more highly oxidized product derived from

He could not even drink freshly squeezed grape juice (*"mishrah* of grapes")[41] or eat grapes or dried raisins (Num. 6:3).

The reason for a Nazirite's separation from anything associated with grapes is not explicitly clear. Freedom from the possibility of intoxication could not be the complete explanation for the avoidance of any grape product; raisins do not cause drunkenness. Perhaps J. Barton Payne best captured the intent of the prohibition when he stated that grapes "stood as a symbol for all the temptations of the settled life in Canaan."[42] Payne's view finds support in the account of the twelve spies who brought back to the Israelites a report of what Canaan was like. Moses was careful to record that two spies carried a cluster of grapes from Canaan between them on a pole, presumably because the size and weight of the cluster precluded one man alone from transporting it (Num. 13:23–27). Here was proof that the land God had promised to give His people was remarkably fruitful.

Along with the blessing, however, came the temptation of focusing more on the gift of the land than on the Giver of the gift. Nothing has the capacity for turning people's hearts away from God faster than prosperity. The Nazirite vow was the Lord's way of drawing His people's attention back to Himself. The Nazirite stood out from the crowd by voluntarily abstaining from the enjoyments to which he was otherwise entitled, simply because he loved God and wanted to be separated exclusively for service to Him. Other Israelites who witnessed the sacrifice of the Nazirite would find

---

ethanol.) Because vinegar came from a fermented source, it was likewise a banned substance for the Nazirite.

[41]The Hebrew word is מִשְׁרָה, which we examined earlier in this chapter.

[42]J. Barton Payne, "Nazirite, Nazarite," in *Zondervan Pictorial Encyclopedia of the Bible*, ed. Merrill C. Tenney (Grand Rapids: Zondervan Publishing House, 1976), 4:392.

unspoken exhortation to make sure that the prosperity of a settled life in Canaan had not robbed them of devotion to the Lord.

It would be good for us to pause for a moment and ask how this Mosaic legislation concerning the Nazirite vow applies to us in the Church Age. Surely as believers we should want to live in a way that demonstrates our undivided devotion to Christ. We ought to desire a lifestyle that is different from the quest for economic prosperity so prevalent in the lives of people in our society. Because the consumption of alcoholic beverages today is so intertwined with a worldly culture that is in rebellion against God, it is entirely fitting for us to demonstrate our devotion to Christ by refusing to participate in such a drinking culture.

The Rechabites

Honoring your parents brings blessing. In Jeremiah 35:1–18 we find another account of people who voluntarily refused to drink *yăyĭn*. The Rechabites were descended from a semi-nomadic group of Kenites (Moses' father-in-law was a Kenite). Scripture first mentions them in relation to Israel's exodus from Egypt (mid-fifteenth century BC). About 250 years before Jeremiah's day, a Rechabite named Jonadab had instructed his descendants never to build houses, plant vineyards, or drink wine.[43] The Lord instructed Jeremiah to bring these Rechabites into the temple, set bowls of wine and drinking cups before them, and command them to drink (Jer. 35:1–5). They refused to drink solely because they were loyal to what Jonadab had instructed them many generations previously (35:6). The Lord used this occasion to draw the attention of His people to their disloyalty to the Mosaic Covenant. Even though God had repeatedly sent His prophets to remonstrate with the

---

[43]See Huey, pp. 312–13.

people, those who should have obeyed God ignored His messengers' warning of imminent judgment. If the Rechabites could obey the injunctions of a human ancestor, then surely one would expect the inhabitants of Judah to obey the Sovereign over all.

The reader immediately wonders why Jonadab would have insisted that his descendants shun wine and city living. "Perhaps Jonadab became repulsed and disillusioned by the corruption and immorality he saw in city life and determined to separate himself and his family from its corrupting influences."[44] Whatever the reason, God rewarded them for faithfulness to their ancestor by promising that there would never fail to be a faithful Rechabite serving the Lord (Jer. 35:18–19). About 150 years after Jeremiah's day, God's blessing was still in effect (Neh. 3:14).

Application of this narrative concerning the Rechabites to our day requires careful meditation. I grew up in a home with unsaved parents, where distilled liquor, beer, and wine were present. My parents drank, but they disdained drunkenness and always partook in moderation. After my parents put their trust in Christ for salvation, however, the alcohol disappeared from our home. They never made an explicit point about why they got rid of it, but I inferred from the removal that they no longer approved of the use of alcohol.

Some Christian parents take a much stronger stand on this issue than mine did. They explicitly teach their children that drinking alcoholic beverages is wrong. They warn of the potentially disastrous consequences of alcohol abuse. They point out that today we have numerous options for the safe quenching of thirst. They maintain that drinking beverages with very low concentrations of

---

[44]Ibid., 315.

alcohol in the ancient context is not equivalent to partaking of alcohol today. They insist that a consistent Christian testimony demands abstinence as the only proper manifestation of separation from the world system that makes drinking the test of peer acceptance. If a person rejects this sort of parental instruction, he turns his back on the principle that Jeremiah 35:1–18 should drive home to the hearts of believers: we must honor our parents.[45] Jonadab's offspring understood the association between obeying their ancestor's commands and honoring him. They were motivated to obey by trusting Jonadab's promise that they might "live many days in the land" where they sojourned (35:7). This promise is quite similar to the command of the Decalogue, "Honor thy father and thy mother: that *thy days may be long upon the land* which the Lord thy God giveth thee" (Exod. 20:12, emphasis added). A Christian who breaks his parents' hearts by engaging in behavior they have strongly warned against has dishonored them. Young adults are sometimes tempted to throw off the constraints of what they have perceived to be an overly restrictive upbringing. But there is no blessing in a failure to heed parental warnings about alcohol consumption.

Kings and priests
Avoiding debilitating influences enhances leadership. The Bible makes the consumption of *yăyĭn* wrong for people in certain positions of leadership. In Proverbs 31:4–5 we find, for instance, that kings are to avoid wine because they might drink and pervert the justice due their subjects. Wine not only slows down physical response times

---

[45]Of course, Christ condemned those who followed "the traditions of the elders" in ways that put them in opposition to the greater commandments of God (e.g., Matt. 15:3; 23:23; Mark 7:8); honoring one's parents has its limits, and continuing in a parent's misguided practice has no merit and may be sinful. But God elevates honoring one's parents by including it in the Ten Commandments, and His rewarding of the Rechabites for their faithfulness to Jonadab's commandment confirms His stamp of approval on it.

but also blunts powers of reasoning. It is wrong for a person with significant influence over other people to do anything that even slightly impairs his judgment.

Priests were also prohibited from drinking wine when they came into the tabernacle to perform their priestly duties (Lev. 10:9). The Lord was so emphatic about this injunction that He warned Aaron and his sons that the penalty for disobedience was death. Since this legislation immediately follows the account of Nadab and Abihu's act of offering "strange fire" before the Lord (10:1–3), "there is more than a hint that Nadab and Abihu profaned the Lord's house because they were drunk."[46] The sacrificial system was complicated and required the full mental capacities of the priests. It is unwise for someone who represents the holy God of heaven to do anything purposely that reduces his leadership ability. This is especially true of parents who must lead their children to adopt a lifestyle that brings glory to God.

The existence of these Old Testament instances of voluntary and mandatory abstention from even the diluted wine of the ancient period is instructive for us today. Modern wine is highly intoxicating, and modern life is generally more demanding of mental prowess. We should be leading people toward greater devotion to Christ and further away from the ungodly world system that Satan controls. Total abstention from alcoholic beverages enhances such leadership.

TÎRÔŠ

Yăyĭn is not the only word the Old Testament uses in referring to alcoholic beverages. The word *tîrôš* (תירוש pronounced *tee·rōsh´*)

---

[46]R. Laird Harris, *Leviticus*, Expositor's Bible Commentary, ed. Frank E. Gaebelein (Grand Rapids: Zondervan Publishing House, 1990), 567.

occurs much less frequently—only thirty-eight times. (See Appendix 2 for contextual clues to the meaning of the word in each of its occurrences.) The KJV translates *tîrôš* using three different concepts in English: *wine, new wine,* or *sweet wine. Tîrôš* is the juice from the grape that flows into the wine vat and soon begins the fermentation process (see Prov. 3:10). *Tîrôš* ultimately becomes *yăyĭn* when fermentation progresses to completion. *Tîrôš* appears in most of its uses along with other agricultural products, such as grain and olive oil, and these items are blessings that Yahweh pours out on those who are obedient to His covenant. The book of Deuteronomy alone contains seven such references to *tîrôš* as a blessing, one of which threatens the loss of agricultural provision if God's people persist in disobedience to His Word (Deut. 28:51). Because the book of Deuteronomy was Moses' last address to Israel before the nation entered Canaan to take the land God had promised to His people, Moses was careful to fortify God's people against the idolatrous viewpoint of the Canaanites. These wicked idolaters thought their worship of Baal, the god of fertility, ensured agricultural abundance for them. The Lord wanted to make sure the Israelites understood that Yahweh alone controls crop productivity. Consequently the Mosaic law specified that *tîrôš* was an essential component of the tithe of the firstfruits of the harvest in thanks for what Yahweh had given to His people (Deut. 12:17–18).

Although *tîrôš* did not contain as much alcohol as fully fermented wine, it did have a sufficient amount to cause drunkenness if a person consumed enough of it. Because grape juice starts fermenting quickly after it flows into the vat, even *tîrôš* could be abused.[47] The

---

[47]"Indeed to drink non-fermented juice was probably possible only briefly, in season, just as grapes were being tread, because fermentation occurred quickly in Israel's warm climate." Jack M. Sasson, "The Blood of Grapes: Viticulture and Intoxication in the Hebrew Bible," in *Drinking in Ancient Societies: History and Culture of Drinks in the Ancient Near East,* ed. Lucio Milano (Padua, Italy: Sargon srl, 1994), 401.

prophet Hosea warned God's people that "whoredom and wine and new wine [*tîrôš*] take away the heart" (Hosea 4:11). The phrase "take away the heart" is a literal translation of an idiom meaning "to cause a loss of understanding." Hosea makes the assertion that idolatry is spiritual adultery and causes a loss of cognitive ability just as surely as alcoholic beverages do.[48]

One usage of *tîrôš* requires special examination. Isaiah 65:8 says that "new wine is found in the cluster." How it is that *tîrôš* can be found in a grape that has not even been crushed yet by treading? Oswalt goes in the right interpretive direction when he states that some of the grapes in the cluster "are obviously bursting with the *juice that will become new wine*."[49] In the next verse God furthers our understanding of the doctrine of the remnant that He will save some day. By figuratively picturing the *tîrôš* as still in the grape, the Lord draws attention to the hidden, but nonetheless existent, righteous remnant in Judah.[50]

'Āsîs

Another word for recently squeezed juice is *'āsîs* (עָסִיס pronounced *ngah·sees'*). This word occurs only five times in the Old Testament and is translated *juice, new wine,* or *sweet wine* by the KJV. (See Appendix 3 for a list of these occurrences.) Just as in the case of *tîrôš*, *'āsîs* carried the potential for producing drunkenness if a

[48]See Thomas Edward McComiskey, "Hosea," in *The Minor Prophets: An Exegetical and Expository Commentary,* ed. Thomas Edward McComiskey (Grand Rapids: Baker Academic, 1992), 1:66.

[49]John N. Oswalt, *The Book of Isaiah: Chapters 40–66*, New International Commentary on the Old Testament, ed. R. K. Harrison and Robert L. Hubbard Jr. (Grand Rapids: William B. Eerdmans Publishing Company, 1998), 645 (emphasis added).

[50]See Edward J. Young, *The Book of Isaiah: Chapters 40–66*, New International Commentary on the Old Testament, ed. R. K. Harrison (Grand Rapids: William B. Eerdmans Publishing Company, 1972), 507. The figure of speech is prolepsis.

person consumed large enough quantities.[51] The prophet Isaiah declared that the time is coming when Yahweh will rescue His people from their oppressors. At that time "they shall be drunken with their own blood, as with sweet wine [*'āsîs*]: and all flesh shall know that I the Lord am thy Saviour and thy Redeemer, the mighty One of Jacob" (Isa. 49:26).

ŠĒKĀR

The final word we will examine in the class of alcoholic beverages is *šēkār* (שֵׁכָר pronounced *shay'·car*), translated by the KJV as *strong drink* in all but one of its twenty-three occurrences, with Numbers 28:7 being the exception. (See Appendix 4 for an analysis of these usages.) The Hebrew verb to which it is related means "to be drunk." Because of this semantic connection, P. P. Jenson postulates that originally *šēkār* was a general word for the entire semantic range of alcoholic beverages. Then as wine made from grapes became popular in Palestine, *šēkār* became a term that referred to any alcoholic drink made from something other than grapes.[52] Marvin A. Powell notes that beer made from the fermentation of grains is well attested in the Ancient Near East as far back as early Sumerian culture. He also questions whether the term *beer* is completely accurate. It is possible that the favorite Babylonian beverage was more like *kvass*, a brew that is only about 0.5% ethanol (about one-tenth the alcohol content of modern beer) and has long been popular in Eastern Europe and Russia.[53] Our modern

---

[51]See Eugene Carpenter, "עָסִיס," in *New International Dictionary of Old Testament Theology and Exegesis*, ed. Willem A. VanGemeren (Grand Rapids: Zondervan Publishing House, 1997), 3:470.

[52]P. P. Jenson, "שׁכר," in *New International Dictionary of Old Testament Theology and Exegesis*, ed. Willem A. VanGemeren (Grand Rapids: Zondervan Publishing House, 1997), 4:113.

[53]Marvin A. Powell, "Metron Ariston: Measure as a Tool for Studying Beer in Ancient Mesopotamia," in *Drinking in Ancient Societies: History and Culture of Drinks in the Ancient Near East*, ed. Lucio Milano (Padua, Italy: Sargon srl, 1994), 91.

notions about certain beverages do not accurately describe what ancient people drank. When a modern reader thinks of beer, he imagines a drink that is approximately 5% alcohol. Powell corrects this errant thinking and commends the idea that ancient *šēkār* would have produced intoxication only if people consumed it in large quantities.

The term *šēkār* appears in the majority of its uses paired with the word *wine* (*yăyĭn*). We have already seen that priests were forbidden to drink wine before they came into the tabernacle to perform their duties. They were also prohibited from drinking *šēkār* (Lev. 10:9). A Nazirite could not drink *šēkār* any more than he could consume wine (Num. 6:3). The Lord asserted that the people of Israel drank no *šēkār* or wine all their years spent wandering in the wilderness (Deut. 29:6). So what is true of wine is also true of *šēkār*. When Eli accused Hannah of being drunk, she asserted that she had consumed neither *šēkār* nor wine (1 Sam. 1:15). We can safely conclude, therefore, that the two words together describe the spectrum of alcoholic beverages available to people in Old Testament times.

CONCLUSION

We have seen that God intended His people to view diluted wine and new wine with very low alcoholic content as a blessing from His hand, just as they appreciated all agricultural products from the land He had given. At a time in history when potable water was not always readily available, beverages with minimal alcohol content provided an alternative means of hydration. We have seen from Proverbs 9:2 that ancient Israelites likely did exactly what later Jews most certainly did: they mixed their wine with water just before drinking it. The term the KJV renders *strong drink* probably had a much lower alcoholic content than modern beer. It is a serious mistake for today's believer to assume that modern alcoholic beverages are equivalent to ancient drinks. *Proverbs 23:29–32 actually prohibits the consumption of both undiluted wine and the fortified wines of today.*

Even though ancient beverages had lower alcoholic content, the possibility of drunkenness was a real danger if a person imbibed heavily enough over a short enough time. The Old Testament contains serious warnings against intemperance. Drunkenness can suspend moral judgment, leading to sin that can affect even future generations. Consumption of alcohol today can quickly destroy a person's awareness of danger and so cloud mental reasoning that obedience to God's Word becomes impossible. Alcoholic beverages are a potential trap, full of poisonous snakes and as alluring as a crafty prostitute.

Alcoholic beverages picture the effects of God's judgment. The picture of a drunk staggering as he tries to walk serves as a metaphor of the massive disorientation, incapacitation, and imminent danger people face as God pours out His wrath on human sin. Just as a drunk has had far too much to drink, so sinners will drain the cup of God's fury down to the very dregs. Someday the universal effects of God's judgment will cause the entire earth to "reel to and fro like a drunkard" (Isa. 24:20).

As an opposite metaphor to judgment, abstinence from alcohol pictures devotion to Yahweh. The life of the Nazirite made him an oddity during the time of his vow. Everywhere he went his long hair and untrimmed beard were a sign for everyone to see that this person had voluntarily kept himself from things other people could enjoy. A king who aspired to fairness and equity kept himself from alcohol. The priest who desired to show his people the way of approach to their holy God never drank alcoholic beverages while serving the Lord. Today's believer likewise should adopt a position of abstinence from alcoholic beverages so that nothing hinders his service.

3

WHAT THE NEW TESTAMENT TEACHES ABOUT DRINKING

The vocabulary of alcoholic beverages in the New Testament is much less varied and developed than in the Old Testament. The main word for wine in the New Testament is *oinos*, corresponding to the Old Testament word *yāyin*. There is also one occurrence of the Greek word *gleukos*, wine that has not completely fermented (comparable to *tîrôš* in Hebrew).

OINOS: THE KEY TERM IN NEW TESTAMENT TEACHING

The Greek word *oinos* (οἶνος) occurs thirty-four times in the New Testament. (See Appendix 5 for contextual indications of the word's use in each of these passages.) Its potential for producing intoxication is apparent in Paul's command, "Be not drunk with wine, wherein is excess, but be filled with the Spirit" (Eph. 5:18). The verb *methuskō* ("to be drunk") is always passive in form in the New Testament but connotes a condition that one has brought on himself.[1] Considering the usual practice of diluting wine with water before consuming it, a person would have had to consume either a large volume of diluted wine in a short period of time or undiluted *oinos* in order to become drunk.[2] In addition to prohibiting drunkenness, Paul states the positive command, "Be filled with the Spirit."

---

[1]See Arndt and Gingrich, s.v. μεθύσκω, 500. The verb form in Ephesians 5:18 is a present passive imperative.

[2]Robert H. Stein, "Wine Drinking," 10–11. See also Stein, "Is New Testament 'Wine' the Same as Today's Wine?" in *Difficult Passages in the New Testament* (Grand Rapids: Baker Book House, 1990), 233–38.

The key to being filled with the Spirit appears in a verse that is entirely parallel to the wider context of Ephesians 5:18. In Colossians 3:16, Paul commands believers, "Let the word of Christ dwell in you richly in all wisdom."[3] The two verses considered together indicate that our capacity for being filled with the Spirit is limited by how much of His Word we can internalize. Ephesians 5:18 clearly forbids drunkenness, but the second half of the verse, in combination with Colossians 3:16, commends taking in as much of the Scripture as we can hold.

Oinos as a Cause of Drunkenness

The New Testament authors (1) mandate temperance in the consumption of wine and (2) allow the use of diluted wine as an alternative source of hydration.[4] Paul told Timothy, "No longer drink water exclusively, but use a little wine for the sake of your stomach and your frequent ailments" (1 Tim. 5:23, NASB). Ralph Earle is right on target when he comments, "It is generally agreed that the wine of Jesus' day was usually weak and, especially among the

---

[3]Both Ephesians 5:18 and Colossians 3:16 begin longer sections that develop exactly the same themes, often in nearly synonymous fashion. Being filled with the Spirit and letting the word of Christ dwell in us richly produce a song in our hearts, thanksgiving, submission of the wife to her husband, love of the husband toward his wife, obedience of children to parents, proper service toward masters, and equitable treatment of servants. It seems proper to conclude that when we are filled with the Spirit, we are yielding our lives to His control by letting the word of Christ dwell in us richly.

[4]Someone might object to the idea that anything with even a small amount of alcohol in it would cause hydration instead of dehydration. Serious runners, for instance, usually avoid alcoholic beverages when they want to stay hydrated. It has been found, however, found that although initial ingestion of alcohol blocked the release of anti-diuretic hormone (ADH)—an essential regulator of the body's water balance—this blockage lessened with time and additional alcohol intake. Rubini found that beer (4% ethanol by volume) ultimately causes hydration because of the relatively large volume of water present. M. E. Rubini, et al, "Studies on Alcohol Diuresis. I. The Effect of Ethyl Alcohol on Water, Electrolyte and Acid-Base Metabolism," *Journal of Clinical Investigation* 34 (March, 1955): 439–47. In the case of ancient wine consumption, dilution at or below the level of modern beer would cause a net hydration.

Jews, often diluted with water. Moreover, safe drinking water was not always readily available in those eastern countries."[5]

It was particularly important for leaders in the church to set a good example in avoiding drunkenness. Paul instructed Timothy that deacons must "be grave, not doubletongued, not given to much wine" (1 Tim. 3:8). The verb translated *given* is a present participle from the Greek verb *prosechō*. The general meaning of this verb is "turn one's mind to" something. It is used here to describe the action of paying too much attention to wine.[6] The qualification deals not so much with the physical craving for alcohol as with the mental preoccupation with it. The term is reminiscent of Solomon's injunction against gazing at wine when it is red and sparkles in the cup (Prov. 23:31). The deacon must not have an inordinate affection for something the devil could use to enslave him. In applying 1 Timothy 3:8 to our day, it is appropriate to require complete abstinence from alcohol for anyone in the office of deacon. The comparatively high alcohol content of modern wine makes abstinence the only proper course of action for those in church leadership.

In the case of the overseer, Paul states the qualification for the office using slightly different terminology. First Timothy 3:3 says that the overseer must not be "given to wine." This phrase translates the Greek adjective *paroinos*, literally "alongside wine." The word describes a person who does not put his cup down until he has had too much to drink. It was possible to keep drinking even diluted wine until one reached the point of excess.[7] It seems startling to us that Paul would have to specifically exclude a person like this

---

[5]Ralph Earle, *1 Timothy*, Expositor's Bible Commentary, ed. Frank E. Gaebelein (Grand Rapids: Zondervan Publishing House, 1978), 381.

[6]See Arndt and Gingrich, s.v. προσέχω, 721.

[7]R. C. H. Lenski notes that "a πάροινος is one who lingers long beside his wine, a winebibber, a tippler." *The Interpretation of St. Paul's Epistles to the Colossians, to the*

WHAT THE NEW TESTAMENT TEACHES ABOUT DRINKING

from being an elder or the pastor of a church, but such lack of self-control is a danger in any era of history or cultural context. In the compelling book *Freedom from Addiction*, Mike Quarles recounts his struggle with alcoholism, even after his salvation while he was a counselor to alcoholics.[8] He knew he was a hypocrite, but his life became a pattern of drunkenness, confession, temporary sobriety, and then back to drunkenness. He tried every program and organization he could find to break the hold that alcohol had on him. Finally, the Lord gave him deliverance, but his story illustrates the reality that even someone in active ministry can be dominated by alcohol. Anyone who is tempted to accept the idea that Christian liberty allows him to consume alcoholic beverages ought to read Quarles's story. Not only does he recount the devastation that alcohol brought into his life, but his wife also offers her perspective with such honesty that I came almost to the point of tears several times in my reading of this book.

Scripture also enjoins women to avoid drunkenness. Paul told Titus to instruct older women to be "in behaviour as becometh holiness, not false accusers, not given to much wine" (Titus 2:3). Here the word *given* is the Greek perfect passive participle from *douloō*, a word that describes enslavement to something.[9] Perhaps a woman would start drinking as a way of dealing with stress and disappointment. What began as an escape valve could then escalate into full addiction to alcohol. Such a condition would be the polar opposite of holy living. Once again, verses such as this are

---

Thessalonians, to Timothy, to Titus and to Philemon (Minneapolis: Augsburg Publishing House, 1937), 585.

[8]"Mike and Julia Quarles's Testimony" in Neil T. Anderson, Mike Quarles, and Julia Quarles, *Freedom from Addiction: Breaking the Bondage of Addiction and Finding Freedom in Christ* (Ventura, CA: Regal Books, 1996), 17–193.

[9]See Arndt and Gingrich, s.v. δουλόω, 205.

best applied to our day as mandating complete abstinence from the highly intoxicating beverages that people now consume.

Oinos as a Picture of Positive Spiritual Realities

The New Testament contains not only warnings against drunkenness but also positive uses of wine as a symbol for certain spiritual realities. At times Jesus used wine and the daily experience of drinking it to illustrate a particular truth. Today it seems strange to us that our Savior would use wine as a picture of anything good. We live in a day when many people drink alcohol for the express purpose of becoming inebriated. The untold misery that alcoholic beverages cause in our day is simply staggering. We must remember, however, that in biblical times people drank diluted wine because they lacked the variety of beverages we enjoy today. This diluted wine in Bible days was associated with water as a means for sustaining life. Neither the beverage consumed nor the reason for drinking it has much equivalence with modern wine or drinking practices, so we must not have modern alcoholic beverages in mind when we read about the way Christ used wine to picture positive spiritual realities.

The spiritual reality of identification with those Christ came to redeem

In Matthew 11:1–19, we find the first instance of Christ using wine to illustrate a spiritual reality. He started by instructing the crowd assembled around Him about who John the Baptist was. He said, "Among them that are born of women there hath not risen a greater than John the Baptist" (11:11). But even this great prophet did not suit the generation of Christ's day. Jesus depicted the people as little children who were never satisfied with God's messengers.[10] These fickle children would not decide whether dancing to flute music was more fun than mourning to funeral music (11:16–17). Nothing pleased them. When John lived an ascetic lifestyle, the Jewish leaders were displeased that he was extremely different from them, and they deemed him possessed by a demon (11:18). But when Christ came eating a normal diet and drinking everyday wine, just like the average Israelite, the leaders accused Him of being a glutton and a drunkard (11:19). We can hardly imagine the grief such an accusation must have caused our sinless Savior.

The spiritual reality that Christ sought to impress on the hearts of His hearers is the identification and closeness of the Lamb of God with the people He came to redeem. Even though the crowd meant it in a pejorative sense, it is indeed true that Christ is "a friend of publicans and sinners" (Matt. 11:19). We can all rejoice in that truth, for none of us would have any hope apart from the reality that Christ died for sinners. John the Baptist's diet consisted of locusts and honey, but Christ's diet was that of the typical person of His day. He was so completely identified with those He came to redeem that seven hundred years previously the prophet Isaiah had even called Him "Israel" (Isa. 49:3). John the Baptist lived according to God's will for his life out in desolate places, but Jesus lived with the multitudes, submitted perfectly to the same demands of the Mosaic law in force for every Jewish person, and took the sins of the world on Himself as He died on the cross.

---

[10]William Hendriksen states the matter well: "It is clear that Jesus is here accusing these critics of being childish. There is a difference between being childlike and being childish." *New Testament Commentary: Exposition of the Gospel According to Matthew* (Grand Rapids: Baker Book House, 1973), 491.

The spiritual reality of new life that transcends Pharisaism

Christ also used wine to represent a new spiritual life that was vastly superior to the old Pharisaic attempt at achieving personal righteousness through fastidious adherence to what they thought the law required. Christ never denigrated the Mosaic Covenant. He even stated that not the smallest letter, or even the smallest part of a letter, would pass from the law until it was fulfilled (Matt. 5:18). Jesus often took the Pharisees to task, however, for their misunderstanding of the law as a vehicle for self-righteousness. They did not understand the true internal intent of various commands. They thought, for instance, that as long as they did not murder someone they had fulfilled the law's demand. Christ declared that the Pharisees were gravely mistaken because the intent of the stipulation went right to the heart: someone so angry with his brother that he would like to kill him is guilty of violating the commandment (Matt. 5:21–22).

The Pharisees misunderstood the nature of fasting. They thought there was something meritorious in denying oneself proper nourishment. Under the influence of Pharisaic teaching, the disciples of John came to Christ and asked Him why His disciples never fasted (Matt. 9:14). Christ answered that the bridegroom's attendants do not fast at such a joyous occasion as a wedding (9:15). A new day has arrived for God's people, a time of joyful union between God and believers. Christ used two illustrations of the incongruity of this new relationship compared with the old Pharisaic legalism. No one would sew a patch of new cloth on an old garment because the new material had not been pre-shrunk. As soon as someone washed the garment, the new material would cause a tear that was worse than the original defect the patch had repaired. Then Christ declared, "Nor do people put new wine into old wineskins; otherwise the wineskins burst, and the wine pours out, and the wineskins are ruined; but they put new wine into fresh wineskins, and both are preserved" (9:17, NASB). Only new wineskins have the elasticity to expand as the new wine continues to undergo the process of fermentation and production of carbon dioxide gas. If a person were to put new wine into old stiff wineskins, they would tear, resulting in the loss of both wine and wineskins. The new wine is a symbol for the joy and blessing of a true relationship with Christ in contrast to the burdensome legalism of the Pharisees.[11]

This same symbolism appears in John's account of the first miracle Jesus performed: transformation of water into wine during the wedding feast at Cana of Galilee (John 2:1–11). The biblical text implies that Jesus' mother Mary was probably related to either the bride or the groom since the narrative opens with the information that she "was there" (2:1).[12] Jesus was invited, and along with Him the disciples came as well. Sometime after their arrival, perhaps even *because* their presence put an additional drain on the provisions of the feast, Mary informed Jesus that there was no more wine. To the modern reader this situation seems to be a minor inconvenience, but it was a significant embarrassment to the groom—and even grounds for possible litigation.[13]

---

[11]Colin Brown summarizes the illustration of new wine in old wineskins by observing that "the Pharisaic outlook is burst apart by the life that [Christ] brings." "Vine, Wine," *New International Dictionary of New Testament Theology*, ed. Colin Brown (Grand Rapids: Zondervan Publishing House, 1978), 3:921.

[12]The Greek verb translated "was" (in the imperfect tense) implies Mary's presence during the preparations for the wedding before Jesus arrived. There is a contrast between this imperfect and the aorist tense that describes how Jesus had been invited. See Leon Morris, *The Gospel According to John*, New International Commentary on the New Testament, ed. F. F. Bruce (Grand Rapids: William B. Eerdmans Publishing Company, 1971), 178, note 10. The assistance Mary rendered would be something a close relative or friend would do.

[13]Morris says, "It is also possible that the lack of wine involved another embarrassment, in that it rendered the bridegroom's family liable to a lawsuit" (ibid., 179). When the wine ran out, people would have to provide their own beverage at their expense. That expense could later be recouped in court.

Mary's report to Jesus about this sad turn of events was most likely a veiled request for Him to do something about it. Jesus' response to His own mother sounds harsh to our ears, but the vocative use of *woman* was actually a form of tender address: "Woman, what have I to do with thee?" (2:4).[14] This phrase, literally "what to me and to you," was used in Bible times to idiomatically express the idea "leave me alone." Tasker suggests that the sense here is, "Your concern and mine are not the same."[15] Mary was focused on rescuing the groom from his immediate lack of provision for the feast, but Christ was concerned about higher spiritual realities. Christ's focus in His earthly ministry was always on His coming vicarious death, which would provide imputed righteousness for mankind. When our Savior talked with the woman of Samaria, for example, she could think only of quenching her physical thirst with water from the well. Our Savior, however, was thinking about what water pictured: "But whosoever drinketh of the water that I shall give him shall never thirst; but the water that I shall give him shall be in him a well of water springing up into everlasting life" (John 4:14).

Christ spent His whole life in single-hearted preparation for His *hour* when His work on the cross that would propitiate the just wrath of God on the sin of man.[16] When our Savior said to Mary, "Mine hour is not yet come" (John 2:4), perhaps He was meditating on the way wine was an appropriate picture of the blood He

---

[14]B. F. Westcott, *The Gospel According to St. John* (1881; repr., Grand Rapids: Wm. B. Eerdmans Publishing Company, 1978), 36.

[15]R. V. G. Tasker, T*he Gospel According to St. John: An Introduction and Commentary*, Tyndale New Testament Commentaries, ed. R. V. G. Tasker (Grand Rapids: Wm. B. Eerdmans Publishing Company, 1960), 60.

[16]Tasker observes, "It is impossible to interpret the words *mine hour* on the lips of Jesus without reference to other passages in the Gospel where 'the hour' invariably refers to the hour of the passion. The certainty that one day that hour would strike would seem to have conditioned, directly or indirectly, all that Jesus said or did in preparation for it" (ibid., 56).

would shed. Indeed, the night before the crucifixion He would say to His disciples as He took the cup of the Passover celebration in His hand, "Drink ye all of it; for this is my blood of the new testament, which is shed for many for the remission of sins" (Matt. 26:27–28).

Undeterred by Jesus' initial unwillingness to meet the need at the wedding feast, Mary commanded the servants, "Whatsoever he saith unto you, do it" (John 2:5). John is careful at this point in the narrative to inform the reader that nearby were six stone water jars of the type that the Jews used for their ceremonial washing, each with a capacity of twenty to thirty gallons. It was the custom of the Pharisees to wash their hands very carefully before every meal with water from vessels like these. In our Savior's dealings with the Pharisees, He offended them by His failure to observe their man-made ordinances. In Mark 7:1–13, Christ strongly remonstrated with the Pharisees about their elevation of traditional ordinances above the Word of God. They were more concerned about washing their hands than they were about obeying the command of the Decalogue to honor their parents. The water jars at the wedding feast, therefore, were a visible reminder of the Pharisees' perversion of the Scripture and their self-righteous, fastidious devotion to manmade religion.

Now Christ commanded the servants to fill these water jars to the brim (John 2:7). John does not inform the reader how full the jars were before the servants topped them off, but for the purpose of the contrast that Christ intended, He wanted the jars completely full. Now Christ instructed the servants to draw out some water and take it to the governor of the feast (2:8). The verb *to draw* is *antleō*, used in the New Testament only here in 2:8–9 and in 4:7 and 15, where the verb is used for the action of drawing water from a well (although there is nothing inherent in the verb's meaning that requires drawing from a well). So the source of the water is left ambiguous: it may have come from either the stone containers or directly from the well that had supplied the water in the jars. Regardless of the water's source, the nature of the miracle as a polemic against Pharisaical self-righteousness is unchanged. Somewhere between the water's source and the governor, something miraculous happened: Christ transformed the water into *oinos* (2:9). A process that would normally take an entire growing season happened instantaneously. Christ bypassed absorption of water from the ground by grapevines, the production of grapes, harvesting by the vineyard workers, stomping of the grapes by barefoot workers, fermentation in the wine vat, completion of the fermentation process in storage jars or wineskins, and careful dilution of the wine to ensure that no one at the feast would become drunk.

When the governor of the feast tasted the wine, he was amazed. Conventional wisdom dictated that a bridegroom should bring out his very best vintage at the start of the wedding celebration. Then, after the guests had consumed enough wine so they did not care what they drank,[17] the bridegroom would bring out the cheaper wine. The governor could not understand why this bridegroom

---

[17]The governor of the feast says that normally everyone serves the good wine first, καὶ ὅταν μεθυσθῶσιν ("and when they have drunk freely") the cheaper quality wine gets served. Although the verb μεθύσκω is the same one Paul uses in Ephesians 5:18 to express the idea of becoming drunk, the verb can also convey the less drastic action of "drinking freely," as it does in John 2:10 (see Arndt and Gingrich, s.v. μεθύσκω, 500). Andre S. Bustanoby likewise notes, "Though the word usually means 'drunk,' it can refer to anything from 'cheerfulness' to gross *intoxication*. If John wanted to leave no doubt that these people were drunk he could have used the word *oinophlugia* (excess, or overflowing with wine) or he could have identified the people as *oinopotes*—drunkards." *The Wrath of Grapes*, 76. Clearly, the Septuagint translators used the verb μεθύσκω in Jeremiah 31:25 to convey the idea of drinking to satisfaction (not to drunkenness).

had saved the best wine until last (John 2:9–10).[18] By turning the water from the jars used for Pharisaic rituals into the best wine, Christ was showing the superiority of His life-giving, atoning blood over the dead legalism of the Pharisees. Christ manifested His glory through this wonderful miracle (2:11).

I am aware that some interpreters insist that the wine Christ created was nonalcoholic. I truly have no desire to pick a fight with my brethren over this issue. Everyone must do the best job he can at the process of grammatical-historical interpretation, always relying on the illumination of the Spirit. At times careful interpreters disagree with one another in their conclusions. My only request is that the reader would follow my line of reasoning and objectively evaluate whether it is persuasive or not.

I maintain that an objective reading of the narrative in John 2:1–11 demands the conclusion that Christ made the same weakly alcoholic beverage that people were used to drinking in Bible times. As an exegete I am bound by what the Scripture actually says, not by what I wish it might say. The governor of the feast was no doubt an expert on wine. He deemed the quality of the water-turned-wine better than (not a different beverage from) the wine already served. Twice the passage tells us that Jesus made *oinos* (2: 9, 10). There is no use of *oinos* in the New Testament that requires the interpretive conclusion that it was unfermented grape juice.[19]

---

[18]It is important to notice that the governor's statement does *not* mean that guests at *this* wedding feast had already consumed too much wine, or that the governor had ever presided over a feast where drunkenness was a problem. Westcott observes, "The words are half playful and fall in with the character of the scene. The form of the first part of the sentence is proverbial, and there is nothing to offend in the strong term *have well drunk* (comp. Gen. xliii. 34, LXX.), 'drunk freely.'" *The Gospel According to St. John*, 38).

[19]Arndt and Gingrich define *oinos* as "wine, normally the fermented juice of the grape" (564). In his comments on 1 Timothy 5:23, Marvin R. Vincent states, "Observe that οἶνος here, as everywhere else, means *wine, fermented* and *capable of intoxicating,*

If John had wanted to inform us that Jesus made grape juice, he would have used the Greek word with that meaning (the word is *trux*). In Arndt and Gingrich's lexicon, the standard source for study of biblical Greek, we learn that "the word for 'must,' or unfermented grape juice, is τρύξ" [*trux*].[20] Likewise, the most respected source for the use of Greek terms in the secular literature of the New Testament era, a lexicon by Liddell and Scott, informs us that *trux* is "wine not fermented and racked off, must." Liddell and Scott list several sources for this use of *trux*: the Tebtunis Papyri, Cratinus, and Aristophanes.[21] Although the term *trux* is not used in the New Testament, it was a viable word the inspired writers likely had in their vocabularies. There is absolutely no explanation for why John would not have used this term if he wanted to say that Christ made grape juice.

The caveat we must keep in mind, however, is that only debauched people drank undiluted wine in Christ's day. MacArthur correctly observes, "Since the strongest wine normally drunk was mixed at least with three parts water to one of wine, its alcohol content would have been in a range no higher than 2.25–2.75 percent."[22] He concludes, "The wine of Bible times was not the same as the unmixed wine of our own day. Even the more civilized pagans of Bible times would have considered the drinking of modern wines to be barbaric and irresponsible."[23] MacArthur comes to the same conclusion in his study Bible note on John 2:3 concern-

---

and not a sweet syrup made by boiling down grape-juice, and styled by certain modern reformers 'unfermented wine.'" *Word Studies in the New Testament* (McLean, VA: MacDonald Publishing Company, n.d.), 4:270 (emphasis original).

[20]Arndt and Gingrich, 564.

[21]Henry George Liddell and Robert Scott, *A Greek-English Lexicon* (London: Oxford University Press, 1925), 2:1830.

[22]John F. MacArthur Jr., *Ephesians* (Chicago: Moody Press, 1986), 237.

[23]Ibid.

ing the word *wine*: "The wine served was subject to fermentation. In the ancient world, however, to quench thirst without inducing drunkenness, wine was diluted with water to between one-third and one-tenth of its strength. Due to the climate and circumstances, even 'new wine' fermented quickly and had an inebriating effect if not mixed (Acts 2:13). Because of [the] lack of [a] water purification process, wine mixed with water was also safer to drink than water alone."[24] The best interpretation of John 2, in my opinion, is that Christ created a wonderful-tasting, virtually non-intoxicating beverage—what Israelites were used to consuming, only better. Any other interpretation incorrectly defines the normal use of the Greek word *oinos*.

Except for those who imagine that ancient people knew how to preserve grape juice from fermenting, the consensus of most writers in the history of the interpretation of John 2 is that Christ made a weakly alcoholic wine at Cana. In a sermon preached on September 5, 1880, C. H. Spurgeon, for example, notes that English wines of his day were fortified with ethanol from the distillation process, making them outrageously intoxicating. He asserts that the wine Christ made was far different, requiring the consumption of large amounts before it could cause intoxication:

> It was wine, and I am quite sure it was very good wine, for he [Christ] would produce nothing but the best. Was it wine such as men understand by that word now? It was wine; but there are very few people in this country who ever see, much less drink, any of that beverage. That which goes under the name of wine is not true wine, but a fiery, brandied concoction of which I feel sure that Jesus would

---

[24]John MacArthur, *The MacArthur Study Bible* (Nashville: Thomas Nelson, Inc., 1997), 1578.

not have tasted a drop. The fire-waters and blazing spirits of modern wine manufacturers are very different articles from the juice of the grape, mildly exhilarating, which was the usual wine of more sober centuries. As to the wine such as is commonly used in the East, a person must drink inordinately before he would become intoxicated with it.[25]

Albert Barnes likewise cautions his readers not to assume that the wine Christ made was like the fortified wines of modern society. He even provides a chart of the alcoholic content of various types of these highly intoxicating wines available in his day, including port (21–25%) and Madeira (19–29%). Barnes maintains that "the common wine of Judea was the pure juice of the grape, without any mixture of alcohol, and was harmless."[26] In context Barnes does *not* mean that ancient wine had no alcoholic content. His statement, "without any mixture of alcohol" means that ancient wines were *not fortified* with distilled ethanol as wine in his day was. So the wine of the biblical period was harmless compared with modern fortified wines. Ancient wine "was the common drink of the people, and did not tend to produce intoxication. *Our* wines are a *mixture* of the juice of the grape and of brandy" (emphasis original).[27] Barnes correctly argues that a proper understanding of the miracle at Cana does not warrant an equation between the wine Christ created and the fortified wines of the modern day.

---

[25]C. H. Spurgeon, "The Waterpots at Cana," in *Metropolitan Tabernacle Pulpit: Sermons Preached and Revised by C. H. Spurgeon During the Year 1880* (London: Passmore & Alabaster, 1881), 26:493.

[26]Albert Barnes, *Notes on the New Testament* (1885; repr., Grand Rapids: Baker Book House, 1956), 195.

[27]Ibid.

Homer A. Kent Jr. mentions the custom of diluting wine with water as an important consideration in interpreting the miracle Jesus performed at the wedding in Cana:

> Some are troubled by our Lord's providing wine. Efforts to treat this wine as unfermented seem contrived and usually unconvincing. It must be remembered that wine was the common beverage at meals in that culture. Drinking water was often impure. Furthermore, wine partaken of as a beverage was often diluted, especially in Roman times. The social evils of drinking in modern America should not be read back into the culture of Biblical times.[28]

In answer to the question of how Christ could make something alcoholic, one only needs to observe that as Creator, our Savior made the very process of fermentation. Fermentation is not a process of death or decay. It is a process of life, and many organisms rely on it—including humans. (See Chapter 5 for a fuller description of how important fermentation is.) There was nothing inherently wrong with the everyday wine Christ made, just as there is nothing intrinsically wrong with anything Christ created.

Oinos as a Picture of Sin and God's Judgment

Wine as a metaphor in the New Testament does not have an unchanging significance; it can picture God's judgment as well as aspects of His salvation. Wine fits the role of portraying the disastrous consequences of God's wrath on sin because drunkenness has such deleterious effects on a human being. It is no wonder, therefore, that wine in the book of Revelation stands for sin and the judgment God brings to bear on mankind. In Revelation 14:8,

---

[28]Homer A. Kent Jr., *Light in the Darkness: Studies in the Gospel of John* (Grand Rapids: Baker Book House, 1974), 48.

an angel announces, "Babylon is fallen, is fallen, that great city, because she made all nations drink of the *oinos* of the wrath of her fornication." This announcement is a combination of two Old Testament prophecies. Isaiah declared, "Babylon is fallen, is fallen" (Isa. 21:9), a repetition that emphasizes the certainty and completeness of the city's destruction. The prophet Jeremiah wrote, "Babylon hath been a golden cup in the Lord's hand, that made all the earth drunken: the nations have drunken of her wine [*yăyĭn*]; therefore the nations are mad" (Jer. 51:7).

All the nations had been willing participants in the wicked religion of worshiping the Antichrist, and all had joined his political and economic empire. John portrays their participation in the Antichrist's kingdom as getting drunk with wine because the nations have joined in a satanic rebellion against the sovereign rule of God that any sober person would avoid. All the nations that have participated in worshiping the beast "shall drink of the *oinos* of the wrath of God, which is poured out without mixture into the cup of his indignation" (Rev. 14:10). Unlike the diluted everyday wine that people normally consumed, sinners will consume God's wrath undiluted.

GLEUKOS: A SINGLE USE IN THE NEW TESTAMENT

The other Greek term the New Testament uses for wine is the noun *gleukos* (γλεῦκος), but it appears only in Acts 2:13. The setting involves the events of the day of Pentecost. Jews had come from all over the world to worship in Jerusalem, and they spoke many different languages. The disciples, who were together in one place, were suddenly filled with the Holy Spirit and began speaking in the different languages of the people who had come to Jerusalem. These foreigners were completely mystified that uneducated Galileans had the ability to communicate in so many languages. But not everyone was amazed. Some observers took this opportunity to impugn the disciples by claiming, "These men are full of new wine" (Acts 2:13). *New wine* (KJV) and *sweet wine* (NASB) are translations of the Greek word *gleukos*. There are two possible meanings for this word: (1) wine that had undergone the initial phase of fermentation but still had a fairly high sugar content or (2) regular *oinos* that had been sweetened with honey.[29] It was obviously intoxicating if consumed in large enough quantities since the mocking crowd sought to explain the disciples' miraculous speech by asserting that they were simply drunk. Peter dispelled their mistaken idea by noting that it was only nine in the morning, far too early in the day for anyone to be drunk (2:15).

CONCLUSION

The New Testament words *oinos* and *gleukos* refer to fermented grape juice with at least a small percentage of alcoholic content. At a time when people lacked the variety of harmless beverages we enjoy today, drinking wine was an option for safe hydration. This option came with clear warnings against overconsumption. Violation of the principle of temperance disqualified a person from holding a position of leadership in the church. Older women also needed to be very careful how much they imbibed because younger women looked to them as examples of Christian virtue. If the New Testament warns against the dangers of diluted wine, then that warning is far more compelling against the undiluted wine of today.

The New Testament also uses wine as a symbol for the spiritual blessings of salvation that God offers in Christ. Because Christ drank the weakly alcoholic beverage of the common people, wine

---

[29]See Richard N. Longenecker, *John and Acts*, Expositor's Bible Commentary, ed. Frank E. Gaebelein (Grand Rapids: Zondervan Publishing House, 1981), 274, n. 13.

became a picture of His closeness to the people He came to redeem. In the parable of the wineskins and the miracle of the water turned into wine, Christ portrayed the new life He offered through His shed blood as superior to the Pharisaic attempt at earning personal righteousness through fastidious adherence to manmade religion.

In a striking contrast with elements of salvation, wine also serves as a metaphor of God's wrath on sin. The book of Revelation portrays sinners in the eschatological future drinking undiluted wine from the cup of God's wrath.

The fact that Christ drank diluted wine *does not justify* the consumption of our much more intoxicating modern alcoholic beverages. Sometimes proponents of drinking today's wine in moderation will assert, "Christ and the apostles drank wine, so I can too." But the modern beverage simply is not comparable to the wine of the first century. Believers today should completely reject the use of modern wine and other modern alcoholic beverages.

4

What We Can Learn About Drinking from Church History

As we have seen in our examination of the biblical words for wine and strong drink, the Scripture allowed the use of these weakly alcoholic beverages in biblical days and condemned drunkenness. Now we transition to a general examination of drinking throughout church history. A broad historical perspective is helpful for understanding the issue of drinking. We find as history progresses that Christians became less aware of the cultural disconnect between ancient beverages and the more intoxicating modern ones. Even some Christian leaders drank undiluted wine and tried to justify their practices from the Scripture. In the modern era, however, many believers have taken a stand against the consumption of any alcoholic beverage.

THE LORD'S TABLE IN THE EARLY CHURCH

Because the early church was composed of many Jewish converts and quickly spread into what is modern Turkey and Greece, it is not surprising that early Christians observed the Lord's Supper with wine that had been mixed with water. The Church Fathers, such as Cyprian (martyred September 14, 258),[1] emphasized the symbolic nature of this diluted wine:

> For because Christ loves us all in that He bore our sins
> also, we see that in the water the people are intended, but

---

[1] Philip Schaff, *History of the Christian Church: Ante-Nicene Christianity* (1910; repr., Peabody, MA: Hendrickson Publishers, 1996), 2:62.

that in the wine is shewn the Blood of Christ. But when in
the Cup water is mingled with wine, His people are united
to Christ, and the multitude of believers are united and
conjoined with Him in Whom they believe. Which union
and conjunction of water and wine is so mingled together
in the Cup of the Lord, that that comixture cannot again
be separated.[2]

Although someone might object that Cyprian may have gotten a
bit fanciful in his identification of imagery, his view is important
for our study because of his commitment to the use of diluted
wine in Communion.

THE USE OF ALCOHOLIC BEVERAGES BY THE REFORMERS

By the time of the Reformation, church leaders no longer recognized the importance of avoiding undiluted alcoholic beverages. In
Luther's day excessive drinking in Germany had reached epidemic
proportions. Although he spoke more vehemently against drunkenness than any of his contemporaries, Luther imbibed alcoholic
beverages in moderation without a qualm.[3]

In fact, Luther, as an advocate of prohibition would be
as much an unhistorical fantasy as Luther the drunkard.
When in August, 1540, he says: "I drink also, but not
every person ought to try and imitate me," when he says
that God ought to give him credit for occasionally taking a
good draught in his honor, and when he writes to a melan-
choliac: "I frequently drink more copiously in order to vex

---

[2] *The Epistles of S. Cyprian*, Library of Fathers of the Holy Catholic Church, Anterior
to the Division of the East and West, trans. by members of the English Church (London:
John Henry Parker, 1844), Epistle 63, sec. 10, 32:189.

[3] Heinrich Böhmer, *Luther in Light of Recent Research*, trans. Carl F. Huth Jr. (New
York: Christian Herald, 1916), 206–8.

the devil," this all proves sufficiently that Luther was by no means averse to a good drink.[4]

That a man of Luther's standing would participate in an activity that had obviously enslaved many of his fellow Germans is difficult to understand. Christians looked to him as an example they should follow. He does seem sensitive to the example he was setting ("not every person ought to try and imitate me"), but his conscience apparently did not bother him enough to lead him to repudiate alcohol. Believers today should not repeat that error by following his example.

Calvin looked at drinking in much the same way as Luther did. He viewed food and drink as a gift from God to be enjoyed by all people. As did Luther, Calvin put great emphasis on the importance of moderation:

> "It is permissible to use wine," he argued, "not only for necessity, but also to make us merry." Christ's provision of an abundance of "most excellent wine" at the wedding in Cana was proof enough of its goodness. Only two conditions should govern wine-drinking: first that it be moderate, "lest men forget themselves, drown their senses, and destroy their strength"; and second, that, "in making merry," they feel a livelier gratitude to God.[5]

The Reformers insisted that drinking, along with good food, produced social enjoyment and an occasion for redeemed people to praise God for His good gifts.

---

[4]Ibid., 213.

[5]William J. Bouwsma, *John Calvin: A Sixteenth-Century Portrait* (London: Oxford University Press, 1988), 136.

While we extol the Reformers for reclaiming the truth of justification by faith alone and the practice of correct biblical interpretation, we also realize that they were coming out of the darkness imposed for centuries by the Roman Catholic Church. Just as the Reformers were not clear about many aspects of ecclesiology and eschatology, they also remained biblically uninformed about drinking. Their attitude toward the moderate use of alcohol negatively impacted several centuries of church history and clearly demonstrates for us that what we decide about this issue can have lasting influence. The decision we make in our generation will have deleterious effects on many future generations if we do not repudiate the use of alcoholic beverages today. We do not diminish the other positive contributions the great Reformers made by noting their errant view on drinking, and we certainly should not perpetuate their error on this point by following their example.

SOCIAL ASPECTS OF DRINKING IN COLONIAL AMERICA

Because many of the New England colonists were Puritans, they brought with them the Reformers' views about consuming alcoholic beverages.

> Puritans had a straightforward attitude toward alcohol: moderate use was good; immoderate use was evil. Most of their European contemporaries shared this view in the seventeenth century, and most of the western world still does today. Thus, in abstract terms, the morality concerning the consumption of alcohol posed no problems to Puritan ideology. Used in an appropriate manner alcohol was socially beneficial, relaxing, sanctioned by Scripture, even healthy. Used in an inappropriate manner, it destroyed body and

soul, ravaged the family and community, and was an abomination in the eyes of God and the commonwealth.[6]

During their voyage to America on the *Mayflower*, the Pilgrims drank beer. To be fair in our evaluation of this practice, we must note that most Englishmen viewed the consumption of water as an unwise practice.[7] Beer continued to be the beverage of choice for most male New Englanders, although hard cider eventually became popular due to ease of production and its low alcoholic content. Although drinking beer was common at home, taverns began to appear widely during the 1660s.[8] Until this time drunkenness had not been a significant problem in New England. Each community had guarded itself carefully to ensure that drinking did not get out of hand, and penalties for inebriation were stiff. Taverns (known originally as "ordinaries") were more difficult to police. Various laws regulated what took place in taverns, but by the eighteenth century an alehouse culture developed that caused many Puritan leaders alarm. Other New Englanders considered taverns to be an important place of social interaction and relaxation. Because there were no hotels for travelers, even those who spoke against taverns could find themselves staying in one overnight for lack of alternative lodging.[9]

THE TEMPERANCE MOVEMENT

Nineteenth-century America experienced some highly significant changes and the problems that went with them. Probably the most important change was the migration of rural farmers into industrial

---

[6]Bruce C. Daniels, *Puritans at Play: Leisure and Recreation in Colonial America* (New York: St. Martin's Press, 1995), 141.

[7]"Recent experience in England also taught the Puritans that water could be hazardous to good health" (Ibid., 142).

[8]Ibid., 143–44.

[9]Ibid., 144–59.

centers of urban commerce and prosperity. The population of the nation's cities exploded, especially as millions of European immigrants swelled the ranks of new urbanites from the farm seeking a better life and enjoyment. Now there was no influence from a concerned local pastor in a small rural church to encourage people in a lifestyle of temperance. Along with the increase of population in America's cities came the availability of large quantities of distilled liquor at the ubiquitous bars. One hundred proof whiskey is 50% ethanol and outrageously more intoxicating than the beer and hard cider that had been popular in colonial days.

Intoxication became a horrible problem in America's urban areas. Drunkenness ruined people's health, cost them the money that should have gone to feed their wives and children, fueled crimes of every sort, and reduced productivity at work. Christian leaders began to notice the cultural disaster that was unfolding before their eyes. Pastors started to preach on the sin of liquor consumption, and many of them banded together to work in concert against this menace that was blighting the lives of so many. Thus the temperance movement was born.

The War Against Distilled Liquor

Perhaps John Wesley was the first high-profile leader to take a courageous position against "spirituous liquors" (distilled alcohol products). In 1743, he included drunkenness, buying or selling distilled liquor, or drinking these intoxicants as sins that the members of his societies must avoid. In 1777, the Continental Congress passed a resolution encouraging each legislative body in the United States to ban the production of liquor. The first formal temperance group in America, the Union Temperate Society of Moreau and Northumberland, was founded in 1808. This was a local movement that encouraged its members to refrain from drinking liquor.

The first national organization, the American Temperance Society, first met in 1826 in Boston. This group sought to advance its stand against liquor by instituting a nationwide campaign. Also in 1826, Lyman Beecher published his *Six Sermons on Temperance*. These messages stirred people from lethargy to an active opposition to liquor. The movement was now ready to make significant gains in membership and national influence.[10]

The War Against All Alcohol

In 1833, the temperance movement changed from one of combating liquor to a force for total abstinence from *all* alcoholic beverages. People began to realize that beer and wine were causing disaster for former alcoholics who had recovered from addiction to liquor. Men such as Moses Stuart, who had written a work in 1830 with the instructive title *Essay on the Prize-Question, Whether the Use of Distilled Liquors, or the Traffic in Them, Is Compatible, at the Present Time, with Making a Profession of Christianity*,[11] stirred people to action. Stuart admits that Jesus and the disciples drank the wine that was common in Palestine in the biblical setting. "As a confirmation of this, I merely make an appeal to the miracle wrought at the wedding-feast in Cana of Galilee, where water was turned into wine for the accommodation of the guests."[12] Stuart also asserts that he knew of no one in the temperance movement who thought that "the moderate drinking of wine, in such a state as it anciently was in Palestine, was considered improper by the great Author of the Christian religion."[13] The key to Stuart's thinking involved the phrase, "in such a state as it anciently was

---

[10]John M'Clintock and James Strong, *Cyclopædia of Biblical, Theological, and Ecclesiastical Literature* (New York: Harper & Brothers, Publishers, 1891), 10:245-46.

[11]Boston: Perkins & Marvin, 1830.

[12]Stuart, 11.

[13]Ibid.

in Palestine," for he notes that it was customary for ancient Jews to mix their wine with water.[14] But modern wines, especially the varieties that are fortified with alcohol (such as Madeira and sherry), were an entirely different question. Stuart knew of many cases where "Madeira, and Sherry, and Port wines, taken at dinner, and in the social circle of the evening, have sooner or later created a thirst for brandy or other ardent spirits, which has resulted in habitual intoxication."[15] Such treatises as Stuart's led many to the conclusion that Christians ought to shun the use of modern wine. So in May of 1833, teetotalers inaugurated the American Temperance Union in Philadelphia to promote total abstinence from alcohol. Over the next forty years the temperance movement sought legislative means on the state and local levels to ban the distribution or sale of liquor, beer, and wine. There were many victories as well as defeats.[16] Temperance advocates realized that the ultimate solution could come only on the federal level.

Prohibition

The Anti-Saloon League, formed in 1895, became the most effective organization for putting pressure on legislators at the national level. This organization maintained that, by conservative estimate, 19% of divorces, 25% of poverty, 25% of insanity, 37% of pauperism, 45% of child desertion, and 50% of all crime in America were directly attributable to alcohol consumption. Various scientific and medical studies appeared in the early twentieth century that aided the Anti-Saloon League's cause by dispelling many of the myths people had long held concerning the supposed health benefits of alcohol. Even wealthy industrialists funded the League

---

[14]Ibid., 13.

[15]Ibid., 28.

[16]M'Clintock and Strong, 246–49.

because of their concern over alcohol's role in lower productivity and absenteeism at work. The DuPonts, Rockefellers, Kresges, and Wanamakers contributed generously toward the League's annual $2.5 million budget.[17]

The Anti-Saloon League might never have been successful in its quest for prohibition, though, without the events of World War I. Just before the war many German brewing companies joined the German-American Alliance, an organization that sought to pre-serve the heritage of German immigrants in the United States and oppose any legislative actions adversely affecting the beer indus-try. Such an alliance was a bad move for companies with names that were obviously German, such as Pabst, Schlitz, and Blatz. Foes of the beer industry capitalized on the extremely negative feelings many Americans had toward the imperialistic ambitions of the Kaiser. As the war progressed, propagandists pictured the German brewers as the murderers of American servicemen and as scoundrels for using precious resources that should have gone into the war effort. "In 1917, the resolution to prohibit the manufac-ture, sale, transportation or importation of alcoholic beverages in the United States was approved by Congress and sent to the states for ratification. It took only one year and eight days for the 18th Amendment to secure the necessary ratification."[18]

The Preaching of Our Modern Forebears

Our Bible-believing forebears contributed significantly to the fight against the misery, domestic abuse, poverty, crime, and loss of health that alcohol abuse causes.

---

[17]Jane Lang McGrew, "History of Alcohol Prohibition," accessed October 24, 2013, http://www.druglibrary.org/Schaffer/LIBRARY/studies/nc/nc2a.htm.

[18]Ibid.

Billy Sunday

Evangelist Billy Sunday preached to approximately 80–100 million people during a career that spanned the years 1896–1935.[19] Sunday was dead set against the liquor industry:

> I am the sworn, eternal and uncompromising enemy of the liquor traffic and have been for thirty-five years. I saw that nine-tenths of the misery, poverty, wrecked homes and blighted lives were caused by booze. I saw it rob men of their manhood and clothe them in rags, take away their health, rob their families, incite the father to butcher his wife and child, rip the shirt off the back of a shivering man, take the last drop of milk from the breast of a nursing mother, send women to steaming over a washtub to manicure their finger nails to the quick to get money to feed the hungry brood, while it sent their father home from their [sic] hell holes, a bleary-eyed, bloated face, staggering, reeling, jabbering wreck while all hell screamed with delight and heaven wept and the angels hid behind their harps. I drew my sword and have never sheathed it, and never will as long as there is a distillery or brewery or a bootlegger or speak-easy on earth. I put twelve states dry before we voted on the Eighteenth Amendment.[20]

Sunday's words express the sentiment of a warrior for Christ. His stand against sin was never difficult to understand or camouflaged by esoteric nuances of expression. He meant what he said and said what he meant. It would be a shame if we, his heirs in the defense and propagation of the gospel, ever fail to issue just as clarion a

---

[19]William A. "Billy" Sunday, *The Sawdust Trail: Billy Sunday in His Own Words*, foreword by Robert F. Martin (Iowa City: University of Iowa Press, 2005), vii.

[20] Sunday, 68.

call against drinking alcohol. The stand we take will affect future generations for good or ill.

C. H. Spurgeon

Charles Spurgeon likewise realized the importance of the stand one takes on the alcohol issue, not only for the current generation, but as well for those who follow. The temperance movement in England during the last few decades of the nineteenth century was robust. Although Spurgeon did not join the temperance movement until the last few years of his life, he became one of its most enthusiastic supporters. Lewis A. Drummond analyzes Spurgeon's position well:

> Spurgeon, well aware of the devastating effects of drunkenness and alcoholism upon many families, regarded alcoholism as a disease people must rid themselves of. It may well have been that after seeing the devastating effects of alcohol, Spurgeon had a dramatic change of attitude. He became a total abstainer and 'donned the blue ribbon' of the temperance movement. Teetotalers would sport a blue ribbon as a testimony to their convictions. This took place in 1887, the year of the Down Grade Controversy, just five years before his death. When he took this stand, it was not because he believed that alcohol was inherently evil—he realized that the Lord Himself had turned water into wine. But he did take his position in the hope that his example would encourage alcoholics, or potential alcoholics, to do the same. He said to a large rally at the Metropolitan Tabernacle, "I don't need it for myself, but if it will strengthen and encourage a single soul among the

5,000 that are here, I will put it on." He would don the blue ribbon and hence take his stand as a total abstainer.[21]

Spurgeon was always concerned about the effect his personal testimony would have on other people. We ought to imitate this biblical quality.

Overly Zealous Proponents of the Temperance Movement

In contrast to Spurgeon's thoroughly biblical approach to the issue of drinking, the temperance movement also included some overly zealous opponents of alcoholic beverages. These men looked at the way the Bible sometimes spoke of wine in a good sense, and other times quite negatively, and concluded that there must be two kinds of "wine"—fermented and unfermented. They felt that the Bible could never say anything good about a drink that had *any* alcohol in it. They thought of alcohol as evil, the product of death and decay. In their zeal to build an airtight case against the consumption of alcohol, they resorted to redefining the biblical words for "wine." They also produced quotations from ancient secular writers, both Greek and Roman, that described what they thought were references to procedures for keeping grape juice in an unfermented state. This assertion that ancient people knew how to preserve grape juice from fermenting sounds strange to us who live after the work of Louis Pasteur, but the idea got its start a little less than a decade before Pasteur did his revolutionary studies.

Eliphalet Nott

The earliest writer I have found who advocated the unfermented-wine theory is Eliphalet Nott. In *Lectures on Temperance*, he asserts

---

[21]Lewis A. Drummond, *Spurgeon: Prince of Preachers* (Grand Rapids: Kregel Publications, 1992), 439-40.

that "the wine that did not intoxicate, and was not used to intoxicate, or *sought to intoxicate*, was good; a blessing was in it. The
wine that did intoxicate, and *was sought for that purpose*, was bad;
it was pronounced a woe and a curse."[22] Nott viewed the word
wine as a generic term. Whether or not it was alcoholic depended,
he thought, completely on the context:

> The good and the evil substances are both entitled logically
> to the generic name of wine, from the obvious fact of their
> common unadulterated origin in the juice of the grape.
> Such, then, would occasionally be the name given to both,
> especially when precision of terms is unnecessary from the
> fact that the context clearly shows which effect, as charac-
> teristic of the respective kinds, was chiefly in view.[23]

There is a certain degree of circular reasoning in Nott's argumentation. Good "wine" is unfermented. If one encounters the word in
a context that involves God's blessing, the "wine" must be, therefore, unfermented.

Nott seeks to convince his readers that ancient people knew how
to keep their grape juice from fermenting. The first method he
discusses is the exclusion of air from the freshly squeezed juice and
the reduction of its temperature. He asserts that "it was a well-
known fact that air and a certain degree of heat were requisite to
fermentation. . . . Hence the Romans were accustomed to put the
new wine into jars, which, being well stopped, new ones being pre-
ferred, were then immersed for several weeks in a cistern or pond;
in fact, as the wine was made about September or October, they

---

[22]Eliphalet Nott, *Lectures on Temperance* (New York: Sheldon, Blakeman & Co.,
1857), xix (emphasis original).

[23]Ibid.

were sometimes allowed to remain immersed during the whole of the winter."[24] Second, Nott thought that boiling the wine to evaporate its moisture content would keep it from fermenting.[25] Third, Nott asserted that the process of burning sulfur in a wine cask would absorb the oxygen and eliminate fermentation.[26] Finally, Nott supposes that filtering the wine to remove its dregs would preserve the fresh grape juice from developing alcoholic content.[27]

Frederic Richard Lees and Dawson Burns

The next important work developing the same ideas that Nott set forth was *The Temperance Bible-Commentary*, authored by Frederic Richard Lees and Dawson Burns in 1870.[28] This is an exhaustive work that analyzes every passage in the Bible dealing with the alcohol question. Lees and Burns did not like the uniform way the translators of the King James Version rendered the Hebrew word *yăyĭn* as *wine*. In an extended chart that covers fifteen pages, the authors offer the translation of the original languages that they think best captures the meaning of verses that deal with "wine." Consider, for instance, the proposed rendering of the verse where *yăyĭn* first occurs in the Bible: "And Noah began to be a cultivator of the soil, and he prepared a vineyard. And he drank of the juice-of-the-grape, and was filled to repletion; and he was uncovered within his tent" (Gen. 9:20).[29] The authors erroneously give the Hebrew word *yăyĭn* the meaning of "juice-of-the-grape" and

---

[24]Ibid., 103-4. Remember that Nott lived at a time when he did not realize that fermentation is anaerobic (taking place in the absence of oxygen). As the chapter progresses, I will show how some have refuted these supposed methods for keeping grape juice from fermenting.

[25]Ibid., 104.

[26]Ibid., 107.

[27]Ibid., 109.

[28]New York: Sheldon & Co., 1870.

[29]Lees and Burns, 397.

link the idea of "filled to repletion" with *šākar* (the verb form of the noun *šēkār* explained on pages 68–69). This work was not helpful to the cause of temperance. Opponents of the movement could now point to the flawed logic, methodology, and conclusions of Lees and Burns and impugn the work of reasonable and accurate interpreters who were fighting against the disastrous consequences of alcohol consumption.

William Patton

The next year William Patton wrote *The Laws of Fermentation and the Wines of the Ancients*.[30] Patton acknowledges his dependence on the works of Nott and Lees and Burns,[31] and his purpose apparently was to produce a more condensed and accessible version of these previous works. Because Patton's book has been reprinted, its contents are much better known to people in our day than the much more comprehensive previous works. Patton recounts several instances of his preaching on the subject of intoxicating beverages. He came away from these experiences with the following conclusion: "I soon found out that the concession so generally made, even by ministers, that the Bible sanctions the use of intoxicating drinks, was the most impregnable citadel into which all drinkers, all apologists for drinking, and all venders of the article fled."

Patton considered this concession unacceptable and set about to study what the Bible teaches. He found three categories of passages on the use of wine: "(1) Where wine was mentioned with nothing to denote its character; (2) Where it was spoken of as the

---

[30]New York: National Temperance Society and Publication House, 1871. In 1874, Patton re-titled the book *Bible Wines: or The Laws of Fermentation and Wines of the Ancients*, published once again by the National Temperance Society. The book was reprinted as *Bible Wines or The Laws of Fermentation* (Little Rock, AR: Challenge Press, n.d. [early 1970s]). Pagination of quotations comes from this reprint edition.

[31]Ibid., 8.

cause of misery, and as the emblem of punishment and of eternal wrath; (3) Where it was mentioned as a blessing, with corn and bread and oil—as the emblem of spiritual mercies and of eternal happiness."[32] From these observations Patton began to wonder whether perhaps there might not be two kinds of "wine" (fermented and unfermented) that could account for the remarkably different categories of usage. "So novel to my mind was this thought, and finding no confirmation of it in the commentaries to which I had access, I did not feel at liberty to give much publicity to it."[33] Indeed, Patton's initial hesitancy was wise, but he later found some contemporaries who agreed with him.

Opponents of the Unfermented-Wine Theory
It did not take long, however, before accurate interpreters began to refute the unfermented-wine theory.

Robert Watts
Robert Watts begins his forty-seven-page refutation of *The Temperance Bible-Commentary* with this aphorism: "When the devil cannot upset the coach [a horse-drawn carriage], he mounts the box and drives."[34] Clearly Watts understands the danger of the unbalanced position in any cause for righteousness, so he painstakingly analyzes and corrects the misinterpretations that abound in Lees and Burns.

A. M. Wilson
The year after Watts's review article, A. M. Wilson published a nearly four-hundred-page refutation of both Nott and Lees and

---

[32]Ibid., 11.

[33]Ibid.

[34]Robert Watts, review of *The Temperance Bible-Commentary*, in *The British and Foreign Evangelical Review* 25 (1876): 14.

Burns.[35] Wilson's book thoroughly dismantled the unfermented-wine theory. Wilson observes with approval:

> Some temperance writers admit that the wines of the Bible were, more or less, alcoholic; that the moderate use of such liquors is in itself lawful, and was anciently sanctioned, when the people were distinguished for sobriety; but they allege that, in the present state of society, when intemperance has become a great national evil, such use is not expedient.[36]

Wilson then notes:

> Rejecting, as above, the plea of expediency, and maintaining the unlawfulness of using intoxicating wine as a beverage, these advanced abstainers [such as Lees] allege that the wines of the Bible were of two kinds: fermented and unfermented; that both kinds were in common use among the ancients, Jews and Gentiles; and that the one is forbidden and the other allowed in Scripture.[37]

Wilson then sets out to prove that the existence of unfermented "wine" at any time in history before the work of Louis Pasteur is a complete myth.

Wilson begins with a survey of the problem of drunkenness in ancient civilizations of Persia, Ethiopia, Germany, Spain, Carthage, China, India, Egypt, Greece, Italy, and Judea. He observes that many of these countries had strict laws against drunkenness, but

---

[35]A. M. Wilson, *The Wines of the Bible: An Examination and Refutation of the Unfermented Wine Theory* (London: Hamilton, Adams & Co., 1877).

[36]Ibid., 1.

[37]Ibid., 2.

none of the laws was enforced. He concludes that wine was "extensively used in the remotest times," that in these civilizations "its free use had developed dangerous excesses," and that the wine they used "was a fermented and alcoholic liquor."[38] Wilson then reasons that if unfermented wine actually existed in the ancient world, it is very strange that no mention is made of such an innocent drink as the solution to the problem of drunkenness. "This fact we take to be a strong indication that, so far as these ancient writers, lawgivers, and philosophers are concerned, unfermented wine is a myth."[39] Wilson can hardly be guilty of employing an argument from silence because the volume of historical material on drinking practices is substantial.

Next, Wilson turns his attention to the process used in making Frank Wright's Passover Wine (the English equivalent of Welch's Grape Juice in the United States). Wilson describes the exacting process of steam heating, both of the juice and the glass flasks which receive the pasteurized juice. He observes that hermetic sealing of the containers better fits "the exact processes of the eminent chemists in their laboratories, than the rude appliances of unscientific peasants in the open vineyards of ancient times." He also points out that even the grape juice preserved from fermentation by modern means immediately undergoes fermentation the moment the lid is removed for only an instant.[40] Wilson insists that because ancient people stomped their grapes in open wine vats, fermentation was unavoidable. "It thus appears that all the expressed juice of the grape, without exception, in ancient times, must have undergone, at least, an initial fermentation."[41]

---

[38]Ibid., 59.

[39]Ibid., 67.

[40]Ibid., 84–85.

[41]Ibid., 88–89.

But what about all the alleged processes that Nott, Lees and Burns, and Patton insist were used by ancient people to preserve their grape juice from fermenting? Wilson now turns his attention to debunking each one.

Filtration. Wilson admits that filtration of the lees was widely practiced in the ancient world and might decrease the alcohol content somewhat—but the wine was still alcoholic.[42] Filtration eliminated sediment and enhanced the flavor of the wine.

Sulfur fumigation. This process is used in the production of modern wine to prevent the formation of vinegar, but ancient authors never said that it prevents fermentation. Pliny is the only writer even to mention it.[43]

Depuration. Regarding the process of removing the impurities, Wilson denies that the Romans added the yolks from pigeons' eggs to prevent fermentation. The process simply produced a higher quality wine. He quotes Horace:

> He who with art would pour a stronger wine
> On smooth Falerian lees should well refine
> Th' incorporated mass with pigeons' eggs;
> The falling yolk will carry down the dregs.[44]

Fumaria. Ancient people sometimes smoked wine in fumaria and blacksmiths' forges to mellow any harshness that existed in the new wine. This process was done to wine that had already begun

---

[42]Ibid., 91–94. A more modern author who makes the same assertion is Bustanoby (38). I do not agree with Bustanoby's discussion of legalism or his accommodating attitude toward the moderate use of alcohol today, but he understands the process of fermentation well.

[43]Ibid., 95. Bustanoby notes that sulfur kills the growth of wild yeast and keeps the wine from developing vinegar content (36).

[44]Ibid., 95–96.

the process of fermentation—not to grape juice in a vain attempt at keeping it from fermenting.[45]

Immersion. Immersion of wine casks in water may have slowed the fermentation process, but it did not prevent it. "The immersion of casks in water, or burying them in the earth, was evidently intended by the ancients, not to prevent fermentation, which, as we have seen, was impossible, but to lessen its activity, to prevent acidity [the production of acetic acid], and to keep the wine cool and sweet."[46]

Inspissation. Wilson admits that ancient people boiled their wine. This process served two purposes: (1) the thickened grape syrup or grape paste made an excellent sweetener and was eaten as food, not consumed as a beverage, and (2) the thickened grape paste had a very high sugar content. This thick paste would be added to the must from grapes harvested during a poor vintage year. The low percentage of sugar in the juice of the poor vintage would be increased for a higher yield of alcohol content in the fermented wine it produced. Wilson notes that boiling wine would remove some of its alcohol since ethanol boils at a lower temperature than water. But the boiled wine would still have some alcoholic content and could not be kept from further fermentation (as long as there was some residual sugar). Wilson insists that the reason ancient people diluted their wine was not because it was a thick paste, but rather on account of the wine's strong alcoholic content.[47]

Many within the temperance movement hailed Wilson's book as a definitive work that presented cogent and irrefutable arguments

---

[45]Ibid., 96–98.

[46]Ibid., 103–6.

[47]Ibid., 108–48.

WHAT WE CAN LEARN ABOUT DRINKING FROM CHURCH HISTORY

against the unfermented-wine theory. C. H. Spurgeon, for instance, included these laudatory comments in a review of Wilson's book in *The Sword and the Trowel* (1877):

> Unfermented wine is a non-existent liquid. Mr. Wilson has so fully proved this that it will require considerable hardihood to attempt a reply. The best of it is that he is a teetotaler of more than thirty years' standing, and has reluctantly been driven "to conclude that, so far as the wines of the ancients are concerned, unfermented wine is a myth.". . . Mr. Wilson has written the thick volume now before us to settle the matter, and we believe that he establishes beyond reasonable debate that the wines of the Bible were intoxicating, and that our Lord did not ordain jelly or syrup, or cherry juice to be the emblem of his sacrifice.[48]

The London Quarterly Review assessed Wilson's book in the 1878 edition. Note especially that the reviewer compares the unfermented-wine theory to a rotten bridge:

> There is no doctrine [such as the unfermented-wine view] too absurd to be held—sincerely and strongly held—by men the correctness of whose reasoning blinds them to the falsity of their facts. The great Temperance movement needs no support from such a dogma as this. A weak argument is like a rotten beam, or a rotten bridge, better removed as soon as it is discovered than left to imperil the multitudes who are trusting to it. We wish all Temperance reformers may accept the arguments advanced in this volume [Wilson's book], but we wish yet more that the people

---

[48]C. H. Spurgeon, ed., *The Sword and the Trowel: A Record of Combat with Sin and of Labour for the Lord* (London: Passmore & Alabaster, 1877), 437.

of England would accept the principles of Temperance reformers.[49]

The Westminster Review had these words of commendation for Wilson's book:

> The author of this work, the Rev. A. M. Wilson, has himself abstained for more than thirty years, and habit and association would naturally incline him to favour the "unfermented theory." Investigation, however, has constrained him reluctantly to conclude that, so far as the wines of the ancients are concerned, unfermented wine is a myth. . . . In our judgment Mr. Wilson has signally triumphed over the champions of the theory which he opposes, abundantly showing that the wines of the ancients, Greek, Roman, Egyptian, and Hebrew, were all fermented beverages, and that such beverages were necessarily used in the celebration of the Passover, the Lord's Supper, and the Agape of the early Christian Church. Victorious as Mr. Wilson really is in his argument, his opponents will of course be of the same opinion still—prejudice, not reason, inspiring the logic which furnishes their conclusions.[50]

The reviewer who contributed an article about Wilson's book for *The Literary World* mentions the controversy that arose over the type of liquid to be used in Communion. He praises Wilson's book as a needed corrective to the overzealous and mistaken views of the unfermented-wine theorists:

---

[49]John Telford and Benjamin A. Barber, review of *The Wines of the Bible: An Examination and Refutation of the Unfermented Wine Theory*, in *The London Quarterly Review* 49 (October 1877 and January 1878): 220.

[50]Review of *The Wines of the Bible: An Examination and Refutation of the Unfermented Wine Theory*, in *The Westminster Review* 108, New Series, vol. 52 (1877): 492–93.

Even a good cause may be weakened when zeal becomes one-eyed and overrides truth and reason. Excellent service, therefore, is done by those who widen the horizon of vision and cast fresh light upon the scene. The high praise of accomplishing this is due to Mr. Wilson, by publishing his much-needed book. He has brought to the task which he set before himself an amplitude of knowledge, that leaves no obscurity where he has trodden, and difficulty unexplained. His abundant materials are well arranged, and his reasonings are acute and forcible.[51]

The final review I quote is somewhat critical of Wilson's book because he simply stated that he was a teetotaler but failed to state reasons why readers should follow his example. The reviewer expresses the conviction that the much stronger alcoholic beverages of the modern period, coupled with the unmitigated disaster such beverages were causing in society at large, mandate total abstinence. Nonetheless, the overall review is quite favorable:

> While we could have wished, for the sake of the temperance cause, to which we are ardently attached, that we could have taken different ground, we were always afraid that our brethren went too far who maintained that all fermented drinks were placed beneath the ban of the word of God. . . . We should suppose that Drs. Lees and Ritchie will find it very difficult to answer this learned and exhaustive volume.[52]

---

[51]Review of *The Wines of the Bible: An Examination and Refutation of the Unfermented Wine Theory*, in *The Literary World: Choice Readings from the Best Books, and Critical Reviews* 56, vol. 15 New Series (Jan.–June 1877): 389.

[52]Review of *The Wines of the Bible: An Examination and Refutation of the Unfermented Wine Theory*, in *The Evangelical Repository: A Quarterly Magazine of Theological Literature* 3, 6th Series (1877): 307–8.

CONCLUSION

Unfortunately, Challenge Press reprinted Patton's book[53] and per-petuated the unfermented-wine view for readers in the twentieth century. Even though Wilson thoroughly decimated the argu-ments that Patton used almost a hundred years before the new edi-tion came out, Patton's ideas sound plausible to some people who are unaware of the historical drama that played out in the 1870s. It seems to some Christians that we must have an airtight defense against drinking alcoholic beverages, so the Bible surely must con-demn any beverage with alcohol in it. One way or the other, we must be able to make the Bible mean what it does not appear to say! Robert P. Teachout, Stephen M. Reynolds and Caleb Butler,[54] and Peter Lumpkins[55] are examples of modern purveyors of the unfermented-wine position. They are just as mistaken as were Eliphalet Nott, Frederic Lees, and William Patton, but the myth of unfermented wine existing in the ancient world yet lives.

History teaches us that we must never approach biblical interpre-tation with an idea in mind of what the Bible ought to say and then set about to make it say what we think it should. The un-balanced position never does any movement any good. The great Baptist expositor John A. Broadus understood this principle well. On November 28, 1894, he wrote a letter to B. W. N. Simms and asserted,

---

[53]Although the reprint edition does not give a date of publication, Google Books indi-cates that it came out sometime during the early 1970s. Schmul Publishing (2005) and Gardners Books (2007) have also reprinted Patton's book. In my opinion, these publish-ers would provide a good service to modern readers by reprinting Wilson's book as well.

[54]Stephen M. Reynolds and Caleb Butler, *The Biblical Approach to Alcohol* (n.p., 2003).

[55]Peter Lumpkins, *Alcohol Today: Abstinence in an Age of Indulgence* (Garland, TX: Hannibal Books, 2009).

The idea that the word *wine* in the Bible sometimes means an unintoxicating beverage is without any sufficient foundation. Some men have written to that effect, but no man who is a thorough Hebrew or Greek scholar, as far as I know, at all takes any such position. It seems to me a great pity that advocates of the great cause of total abstinence should take up so utterly untenable a position. The pure wine of Palestine, in our Lord's time, taken as was the custom with a double quantity of water (a man who "drinks unmixed," among the Greeks, meant a hard drinker), and used in moderation, was about as stimulating as our tea and coffee, and was used by the Saviour and by others just as we use them. The case is altered now, for such pure and mild wines would be very hard to get, and they are not needed because we have tea and coffee, and their use would tend to encourage the use of distilled liquors, which are so much more powerful and dangerous. Therefore it is better to abstain from the use of wine for our own sake and as an example to others.[56]

Most Christians respond to teaching from the Scripture that is based on sound exegesis and applied with correct exposition. We do not need myth for persuasion. Just as in the days of the temperance movement, reasonable people are persuaded to shun alcoholic beverages when they are shown that modern drinks are much more intoxicating than ancient wine diluted with water, that the Bible warns believers about the dangers of alcohol consumption and its potential enslavement, that the example we set for others is crucial, and that we must evidence a Christian love that abhors even the possibility of leading someone into sin.

---

[56]John A. Broadus cited in Archibald Thomas Robertson, *Life and Letters of John Albert Broadus* (Philadelphia: American Baptist Publication Society, 1910), 426–27.

5

The Medical Perspective
on Alcohol Consumption[1]

Christians ought to care deeply about how they treat their bodies. Because our bodies are the temple of the Holy Spirit (1 Cor. 6:19), we must make sure that we are not doing anything that would be harmful to our long-term health. Sometimes medical science changes its conclusions about various issues related to nutrition and health. When I was growing up, the prevailing wisdom dictated the use of margarine instead of butter. Medical researchers later found that the trans fats in margarine were bad for the heart. Suddenly butter was back on the table. Some matters, however, are quite assured due to unassailable research and unanimous opinion. One such issue is smoking. Many statistical studies have identified smoking as the primary cause of several serious lung diseases, including lung cancer and chronic obstructive pulmonary disease (COPD). These ailments kill hundreds of thousands of people every year.[2] Smoking is also well known to be a major contributor to many other cancers and to the cardiovascular disease process. The evidence is so overwhelming that only an extremely ill-informed or ill-willed person would deny the cause-and-effect relationship. These days it would be unusual to find a Christian who thinks he can smoke and still be a good steward of his body.

---

[1] This chapter was written in collaboration with Daniel T. Borkert, MD. I am indebted to him for his editorial review and addition of helpful material. I would also like to thank Michael Gray, PhD, of the biology department at Bob Jones University for reviewing the chapter.

[2] "Tobacco Facts," National Cancer Institute, accessed October 21, 2013, http://www.cancer.gov/cancertopics/smoking.

On the other hand, most of us have heard about certain studies on the benefits of moderate drinking and have wondered if consuming alcoholic beverages is beneficial to a person's health. An examination of the current views of medical researchers is necessary to determine whether or not a person can consume alcoholic beverages and be a good steward of his body. I maintain that proper Christian stewardship necessitates a repudiation of drinking modern alcoholic beverages.

A Scientific Assessment of Fermentation

We must be careful not to accept erroneous arguments in making the decision to shun alcohol. Some well-meaning authors who conclude that abstinence from alcoholic beverages is the correct position are unfortunately guilty of promulgating inaccuracies about the process of fermentation. They view fermentation as a process of death and decay and therefore argue that consuming anything that is the product of fermentation is harmful to human health. Peter Lumpkins, for example, asserts that fermented wine is deteriorated wine.

> What many fail to realize is that the natural fermentation of grapes does not lead to a drinkable beverage. Instead, uncontrolled it leads to a product unfit to consume. Natural fermentation is the second law of thermodynamics applicable to crushed grapes. Fermenting wine produces the horrid, foul odor of rot and decay—a particularly formidable challenge the ancients combatted. The fermentation process was carefully monitored and controlled, else the only product resulting would be soured vinegar impossible to drink.[3]

---

[3]Lumpkins, 113.

One hardly knows where to start in refuting this series of inaccurate statements. First, natural fermentation leads to a beverage that people have been consuming for thousands of years. It is eminently drinkable, and it does not smell like rot or decay. If it smelled like death in a bottle, there would be no need for a book that argues for abstinence from such a class of horrible drinks!

Second, Lumpkins seems to misunderstand the second law of thermodynamics. The second law essentially states that no heat engine can operate continuously with 100% efficiency. This means it always produces waste heat that increases the entropy of its environment. Think of entropy as a measure of randomness. A heat engine converts heat energy to mechanical energy. Heat engines can be inanimate machines or living beings. Humans are one type of heat engine. We eat food, digest it, and produce heat energy by oxidizing digestion products so that we can utilize the mechanical energy that allows us to go about our daily activities. Respiration produces carbon dioxide gas and water vapor, and these waste products exist at a higher entropy level than the food we consumed. We are little thermal polluters who are increasing the entropy of the world! So are all living organisms, including yeast.

The production of ethanol is through the metabolic pathways of yeasts. These are living organisms that thrive on fermentation, a process they use for life. Vinegar (acetic acid) is the product of bacterial oxidation of the ethanol that yeasts produce by fermentation. The ancients battled the bacterial oxidation of ethanol, not fermentation itself.

Bacteria and yeasts use fermentation pathways to produce many of the foods that have been staples of human nutrition for millennia. The same fermentation pathway that produces ethanol and carbon dioxide in fruit juices causes bread to rise. (Ethanol is baked out in the oven.) Cheese is also a product of fermentation. Bacteria in the human digestive system utilize fermentation, and they are essential for the proper functioning of the digestive system. The Lord built into our muscle tissue the ability to generate energy in the absence of adequate oxygen. If our level of muscular exertion exceeds our body's ability to deliver oxygen to the muscles, the only option left to generate the needed energy is fermentation. We have all suffered from the aftermath of this fermentative process—lactic acid buildup that produces muscle soreness.[4] There are times, however, when our very lives might depend on fermentation. Being able to run away from a dangerous situation when we are short of breath more than compensates for any muscle soreness we experience.

Fermentation is essential for the survival of microorganisms that live in anaerobic (lacking oxygen) environments, for the production of some of the basic foods we enjoy, and for muscular activity when the available oxygen is inadequate for aerobic respiration. We should never argue against alcohol consumption on the basis of a faulty understanding of fermentation. Fermentation is a process of life, not death. It is an integral part of the world that God created.

THE MEDICAL VIEW OF ALCOHOL ABUSE

Now that we have a proper perspective on fermentation, we can examine the extensive research that medical science has conducted on the health issues involved in abusing alcohol, a product of fermentation. Some conclusions about the effects of alcohol on the

---

[4]Some sources call this process anaerobic respiration, but this is not an appropriate label. Because the waste products (lactic acid) are organic, this process is properly termed fermentation. This is analogous to the ethanolic fermentation in yeast and differs only in the nature of the waste products produced.

human body are certain, and some are more tentative. The most obvious and undeniable physiological effect is on the function of the human brain. Excessive consumption of alcohol produces serious psychological problems according to *U.S. News & World Report*: "For active alcoholics, drinking trumps reason. It distorts judgment. It severs the connection between behavior and consequence. It lays waste to marriages, friendships, and careers. It leaves children stranded. For alcoholics, love and logic can't hold a candle to liquor."[5]

Medical researchers are just beginning to understand the biochemical mechanisms that produce addiction to alcohol. Alcohol has the ability to affect the brain by stimulating centers of behavior and learning. In response to alcohol, the brain releases GABA, a neurotransmitter that produces powerful feelings of euphoria. At the same time the brain also releases glutamate to counterbalance the influence of GABA. Glutamate joins GABA in certain areas of the brain that control memory. In order to deal with excess amounts of glutamate, the brain responds by changing the structure of receptor cells, but habitual use of alcohol negates the brain's response. Eventually the combination of GABA and high levels of glutamate produces such strong memories of the euphoria of drinking that the alcohol abuser who has attempted to recover from his addiction may find an overwhelming urge to drink even years after he has avoided any alcoholic beverages.[6] *BusinessWeek* reports that "sophisticated brain-imaging technologies have demonstrated that constant use of alcohol significantly alters the

[5]Susan Brink, "Your Brain on Alcohol," *U.S. News & World Report*, April 29, 2001, http://www.usnews.com/usnews/culture/articles/010507/archive_001356_2.htm.
[6]Catherine Arnst, "Can Alcoholism Be Treated?" *BusinessWeek,* April 11, 2005, 97.

structure of the brain in ways that can last for months and even years, creating a chronic brain disease."[7]

It is hard to imagine that anyone who consumes alcohol took his first drink with the specific goal of becoming an alcoholic. Indeed, there is no way of predicting with any degree of certainty who might become an addict. Researchers at Washington University School of Medicine have found, however, that the earlier people start drinking, "the greater the risk for alcohol dependence and the more prominent the role played by genetic factors."[8] There are approximately 18 million people in the United States who abuse or are addicted to alcohol (about 6% of the total population). Out of this total, only about 2 million abusers of alcohol seek treatment each year, and about 90% of them will suffer a relapse within four years.[9]

Clearly the physiological and psychological effects of excessive alcohol consumption are horrendous. Each year one hundred thousand Americans die from problems related to alcohol.[10] More specifically, 33% of suicides, 50% of homicides,[11] 39% of traffic fatalities,[12] and between 48% and 68% of deaths from fire are the direct consequence of alcohol impairment.[13] These statistics relate only the deaths involved; there are hundreds of thousands more

[7]Ibid., 96.

[8]"First Drink Influences Alcoholic Genes," *Laboratory Equipment*, accessed September 21, 2009, www.laboratoryequipment.com/news-drinks-influences-alcohol-genes-092109.aspx.

[9]Arnst, 97.

[10]"Alcoholism," Mayo Clinic, accessed June 14, 2010, http://www.mayoclinic.com/health/alcoholism/DS00340.

[11]"Sobering Facts on the Dangers of Alcohol," *NY Newsday*, April 24, 2002.

[12]"Alcohol Impairment," National Highway Traffic Safety Administration, accessed June 14, 2010, http://www.nhtsa.gov/Research/Human+Factors/Alcohol+Impairment.

[13]"Position Paper on Drug Policy: Physician Leadership on National Drug Policy (PLNDP)," Brown University Center for Alcohol and Addiction Studies, 2000, accessed October 28, 2013, http://www.plndp.org/Resources/researchrpt.pdf.

who are injured through the use of this legal drug. In fact, one fourth of all emergency room admissions are related to alcohol.[14]

Besides trauma, many other harmful physical manifestations come from drinking alcohol. Most people are aware of the gastrointestinal diseases of hepatitis, gastritis, cirrhosis, and pancreatitis that accompany chronic alcohol abuse.[15] But alcohol use may also lead to the development of a number of other acute and chronic diseases. Many of the neurological problems of dementia, stroke, and neuropathies are the result of drinking.[16] Some cardiac ailments, including myocardial infarction (heart attacks), cardiomyopathies, hypertension, and atrial fibrillation, are a direct consequence of the consumption of alcohol.[17] Finally, many cancers of the mouth, throat, esophagus, stomach, liver, prostate, and breast are linked to even moderate use of alcohol.[18] When the costs of medical treatment, lost wages, and law-enforcement resources are all added up, alcohol addiction costs Americans $185 *billion* per year.[19] (That's over $600 per year for every man, woman, and child in America.) When considering all these facts together, any reasonable individ-

---

[14]"Sobering Facts."

[15]"Quick Stats: General Information on Alcohol Use and Health," Centers for Disease Control and Prevention, accessed June 14, 2010, http://www.cdc.gov/alcohol/quickstats/general_info.htm.

[16]G. Carrao et al., "A Meta-analysis of Alcohol Consumption and the Risk of 15 Diseases," *American Journal of Preventive Medicine* 38 (2004): 613–19.

[17]J. Rehm et al., "Alcohol-related Morbidity and Mortality," *Alcohol Research and Health* 27 (2003): 39–51.

[18]"Consumption of wine, beer, hard liquor, and all combined showed positive associations with neoplasms of the oral cavity, larynx, esophagus, colon, rectum, breast, and thyroid gland." R. R. Williams and J. W. Horm, "Association of Cancer Sites with Tobacco and Alcohol Consumption and Socioeconomic Status of Patients: Interview Study from the Third National Cancer Survey," abstract, accessed June 14, 2010, http://www.ncbi.nlm.nih.gov/sites/entrez?Db=pubmed&Cmd=ShowDetailView&TermToSearch=557114&ordinalpos=25&itool=EntrezSystem2.PEntrez.Pubmed.Pubmed_ResultsPanel.Pubmed_RVDocSum.

[19]Arnst, 97.

ual should be "sobered" to realize that we should not view the consumption of alcoholic beverages as simply a social preference!

The economic costs are just a fraction of the misery. How can we quantify the grief a drunk driver can cause a family whose beloved relative has just been killed in a violent car crash? What value can we place on the life of a woman whose drunken husband just shot her dead in a fit of alcoholic rage? How can we assess the emotional trauma of a child who goes to bed each night terrified that his drunken parent might do him harm?

There is a strong genetic predisposition for alcohol addiction. Of the many scientific studies that could be cited, Megan K. Mulligan et al. conclude,

> Much evidence from studies in humans and animals supports the hypothesis that alcohol addiction is a complex disease with both hereditary and environmental influences. Molecular determinants of excessive alcohol consumption are difficult to study in humans. However, several rodent models show a high or low degree of alcohol preference, which provides a unique opportunity to approach the molecular complexities underlying the genetic predisposition to drink alcohol.[20]

A Christian can carry the same genetic risks that any unsaved person carries. The same biochemical factors that enslave unsaved people are at work in a Christian's brain when he drinks alcoholic beverages. It would be naive for a believer to think that the

---

[20]Megan K. Mulligan et al., "Toward Understanding the Genetics of Alcohol Drinking through Transcriptome Meta-analysis," *Proceedings of the National Academy of the Sciences of the United States of America* 103 (16) (April 18, 2008): 6368–73, http://www.ncbi .nlm.nih.gov/pmc/articles/PMC1458884.

Lord will somehow protect him from alcoholism simply because he is regenerate. Alcoholism is definitely a spiritual problem, and Scripture repeatedly condemns it as sin (see, e.g., 1 Cor. 6:9–10). But alcoholism has the additional dangerous aspect of physical addiction. Drinking alcoholic beverages is the medical equivalent of playing Russian roulette with a real handgun loaded with real bullets. It is a sin against the Lord who made us stewards of our bodies to flirt with danger like this.

Because the modern believer has easy access to the results of research showing the addictive mechanisms of alcohol use, *he is completely without excuse for even starting down a course that can lead to enslavement.* There is no chance of addiction to alcohol for the Christian who never takes his first drink. The correct scriptural stance is to repudiate anything that might gain the mastery over a believer's life (1 Cor. 6:12). Today's Christian enjoys dozens of options for safe beverages to drink, unlike a person during biblical times. There are *no* compelling reasons to justify drinking today and *many* reasons to cause the wise believer to stay as far away as he can from becoming ensnared by the mind-altering potential of alcohol.

THE RISKS OF MODERATE ALCOHOL CONSUMPTION

Someone who realizes the danger of alcohol abuse might be open, however, to the erroneous idea that the potential health benefits of moderate alcohol consumption outweigh the risks. Indeed many of the medical decisions we make balance certain risk factors against health benefits. Research in the area of alcohol usage indicates that *moderate* alcohol intake can actually be helpful in preventing cardiovascular disease. When alcohol is consumed at the proper dose, it appears, among other things, to raise good cholesterol (HDL), lower blood pressure, and inhibit platelet function in accelerating arteriosclerosis. This cardio-protective effect is inherent to the ethanol molecule alone and is independent of the type of alcoholic beverage.[21]

Lest a person make the wrong decision in his risk assessment of the benefits of moderate alcohol consumption, however, it is important to note that medical experts do *not* conclude that the potential benefits of moderate alcohol use outweigh the risks. Medical researchers realize that some people are going to drink no matter how strongly doctors warn against deleterious effects. The same phenomenon occurs with smoking. Even though each pack of cigarettes contains a strong warning that the contents are carcinogenic, people still light up and puff away on a ticket to an early date with a coffin! Because medical practitioners know that many people will drink no matter how stern their warnings, they seek to convince those who already drink to do so moderately. For those who heed their advice, some health benefits may accrue. But it would be wrong for Christians to follow the same advice given to people who incur great risk to their lives and well-being by drinking in the first place.

Anyone who has been reading health-advice articles in magazines and newspapers has undoubtedly seen at least one presentation of the benefits of limited alcohol consumption. *Science News*, for example, included the item, "Alcohol Answer? Drinks Lower Glucose to Protect Heart." This article postulates a mechanism by which ethanol protects the heart from disease. Any alcoholic drink, including wine, beer, or gin, lowers spikes in glucose levels (without producing higher levels of insulin). Since high levels of blood glucose are deleterious to heart health, moderate alcohol

---

[21]"Red Wine and Resveratrol: Good for Your Heart?" Mayo Clinic, accessed October 21, 2013, http://www.mayoclinic.com/health/redwine/HB00089.

consumption helps to protect against type-2 diabetes and cardio-vascular disease.[22]

The most important consideration in news like this is that *no research article I have read advises people who do not currently drink to start drinking*. It would be irresponsible to recommend a behavior that could possibly lead to the development of alcohol abuse, along with its destruction of health and even life. Clearly there are much better ways of dealing with heart disease and type-2 diabetes than drinking alcohol in moderate quantities. Daily exercise, regulation of caloric intake with attendant weight loss, avoidance of foods with high levels of refined carbohydrates, increased intake of whole grains and fiber, regular visits to a doctor, and use of appropriate medication are all far superior to consuming alcohol in dealing with the problem of impaired glucose metabolism. The believer must look at health as a complete lifestyle issue, and that mindset rejects trying to procure possible health benefits from drinking—no matter how moderate the intake of ethanol might be.

Some articles on the benefits of limited wine consumption identify the antioxidant resveratrol as the substance in red wine that provides cardiovascular benefit. Resveratrol (3,4,5-trihydroxystilbene) occurs naturally in grapes, red wine, and peanuts. Most of the studies on resveratrol to date have involved *in vitro* lab work, not controlled studies in humans. One downside of the chemical is its possible promotion of human breast cancer cell development.[23] Unfermented grape juice contains resveratrol, and it is available as

[22]"Alcohol Answer? Drinks Lower Glucose to Protect Heart," *Science News,* June 30, 2007, 405.

[23]Stephen Barrett, "Resveratrol: Don't Buy the Hype," accessed October 21, 2013, http://quackwatch.com/01QuackeryRelatedTopics/DSH/resveratrol.html.

a nutritional supplement, so drinking red wine is unnecessary if a person wishes to include this antioxidant in his diet.

Conclusion

The Harvard School of Public Health, like many reputable medical websites, maintains that there are proven health benefits of moderate alcohol consumption (one or two drinks per day for men, one for women) in fighting cardiovascular disease and in improving the body's ability to metabolize glucose. For younger adults, however, the risks of possible addiction outweigh any potential benefits. Women over sixty with a history of heart disease in their families might benefit from moderate alcohol intake, but they must realize that their chance of developing breast cancer would increase. Men over sixty who are at higher risk for heart disease might also benefit from one or two drinks per day. These benefits, however, come with a warning: "Given the complexity of alcohol's effects on the body and the complexity of the people who drink it, blanket recommendations about alcohol are out of the question."[24] In other words, *these medical experts simply do not recommend that people start drinking moderately in order to achieve heart health.*

Because of the very real possibility of addiction and its associated physical and social ills, consuming alcohol for its medicinal benefit is neither necessary nor prudent.[25] Instead of drinking, there are vastly superior ways for people to increase their overall health and avoid cardiovascular disease. If someone is leading a sedentary lifestyle, the first step toward improved health involves getting some sort of daily exercise. Proper nutritional choices are also impor-

---

[24]"Alcohol: Balancing Risks and Benefits," Harvard School of Public Health, accessed April 3, 2014, http://www.hsph.harvard.edu/nutritionsource/alcohol-full-story.html.

[25]This is true even in the use of wine as an analgesic (cf. Prov. 31:6). Modern medicine offers pain medications that are far more effective and less risky than alcohol.

tant. Good cardiovascular health must be the result of wise life-style changes—not from the consumption of alcoholic beverages.

6

HOW DRINKING IS INCOMPATIBLE
WITH HOLINESS

Ultimately the choices we make in life should not be based primarily on medical considerations, the example of what our friends are doing, or what a popular blogger on the Christian scene is advocating. Everything a Christian does should be the result of his or her desire to love and honor Christ. We have been called to a life of sanctification. Sanctification is a lifelong process of increasing conformity to the image of Christ (Rom. 8:29), and that image involves holiness. Growth in personal holiness ought to determine everything we are internally and everything we do externally.

HOLINESS HAS A POSITIVE FOCUS ON GOD

Holiness is the word God has chosen in divine revelation to communicate the totality of His being. Out of all the descriptions of holiness I've read, I like this one by A. S. Wood the best:

> Holiness is not merely one of God's attributes. It represents His essential nature. Holiness is His selfhood. When He swears by His holiness, He swears by Himself (Amos 4:2; 6:8; cf. Gen. 22:16; Ps. 89:35; 108:7). . . . It expresses *His whole divine personality.*[1]

Wood bases his definition on an interesting comparison of Amos 4:2 with 6:8. These two parallel verses declare that God takes an

---

[1] A. S. Wood, "Holiness," *Zondervan Pictorial Encyclopedia of the Bible*, ed. Merrill C. Tenney (Grand Rapids: Zondervan Publishing House, 1976), 3:175 (emphasis added).

oath that judgment is coming on His people. Amos 4:2 says that the certainty of judgment is predicated on God's holiness: "The Lord God hath sworn by his holiness." In parallel manner, Amos 6:8 reveals that His *nephesh* ensures the fulfillment of what He promises: "The Lord God hath sworn by himself [literally, His *nephesh*]." The association of the word *holiness* with *nephesh* is important because the Old Testament uses the Hebrew word *nephesh* in referring to the totality of a person's being. Taken together, the two verses seem to indicate that God's holiness is the totality of His being. In Isaiah's vision of the Lord sitting on His throne (Isa. 6), out of all the terms the seraphs could have used to describe who God is, these angelic beings chose to use the word *holy* in an emphatic, three-fold repetition.

Logically, then, conformity to the image of Christ involves growth in holiness, the transformation of the believer's character into a finite reflection of the infinite aspects of God's being. We will never be divine, but God is working to turn conditions back to mankind's existence in the Garden of Eden before Adam and Eve fell into sin and death. This is sanctification, and it is foundationally a positive concept that entails becoming more like our Savior. As we read the Bible in search of what God has revealed about Himself, the Holy Spirit uses Scripture to transform our character. This process of sanctification, then, requires the combination of the Christian's highest diligence in the study of the Word and the Lord's supernatural grace.

Another positive aspect of sanctification is the believer's devotion to God and His will. The Old Testament describes even inanimate objects as holy in this sense of being devoted entirely for God's use. Consider, for example, the holy status of all the wealth in the city of Jericho. Joshua carefully instructed his fellow Israelites that everything in the city was devoted[2] to the Lord (Josh. 6:18). Consequently no Israelite was to keep any wealth for himself: "All the silver, and gold, and vessels of brass and iron, are consecrated unto the Lord: they shall come into the treasury of the Lord" (6:19). The word translated *consecrated* is the Hebrew noun for holiness. The verse literally says, "All the silver, and gold, and vessels of brass and iron, are holiness to Yahweh." This passage teaches that the term for something that has been devoted exclusively for the Lord's use is synonymous with what is holy. Achan unwisely chose not to follow Joshua's instructions. He saw some clothing, silver, and gold and took the items for his own use. His choice proved fatal (7:19–26). When the Lord determines that something is devoted to His use exclusively, He does not tolerate the abrogation of His will.

Throughout the Old Testament God declares that He has chosen Israel to be holy in this sense of being completely devoted to loving and obeying Him. Right after obtaining their freedom from Egyptian enslavement, for example, the Israelites came to Mount Sinai and received this declaration from the Lord: "If ye will obey my voice indeed, and keep my covenant, then ye shall be a peculiar treasure unto me above all people: for all the earth is mine: and ye shall be unto me a kingdom of priests, and an holy nation" (Exod. 19:5–6). The word translated *peculiar treasure* (Heb. *segullah*) refers not to something odd or unusual but to what is most highly treasured.[3] Israel had an almost unbelievably privileged position,

---

[2]The Hebrew word is *ḥērēm*, translated by the KJV as *accursed* or *accursed thing*. The idea is something that has been devoted to the Lord for whatever He purposes, whether total annihilation or exclusive use. See Leon J. Wood, חרם," *Theological Wordbook of the Old Testament*, ed. R. Laird Harris (Chicago: Moody Press, 1980), 1:324–25.

[3]E. Lipinski notes that the term "implies both Yahweh's initiative and his personal engagement. This kind of acquired possession is valued more highly, and the word ultimately becomes the designation for any possession that one especially values." "סְגֻלָּה," *Theological Dictionary of the Old Testament*, ed. G. Johannes Botterweck, Helmer

but the nation never experienced the blessings of this status because the people were unfaithful to the stipulations of the promise. In fact, Israel did not obey God's voice and refused to obey His covenant. They were not a holy nation because they turned from devotion to God.

God has commissioned the church to experience what Israel failed to enjoy. In a wonderful example of the continuity between the Old and New Testaments, Peter makes it clear that we must fulfill what Israel never did:

"But ye are a chosen generation, a royal priesthood, *an holy nation*, a peculiar people; that ye should show forth the praises of him who hath called you out of darkness into his marvelous light: which in time past were not a people, but are now the people of God: which had not obtained mercy, but now have obtained mercy" (1 Pet. 2:9–10; emphasis added).

Our transformed lives of devotion to Christ must be a continual display of God's holiness to unsaved people around us.

HOLINESS MANDATES A NEGATIVE RESPONSE TO THE WORLD SYSTEM

When Christians who are growing in holiness encounter the world system, however, the concept of holiness takes on a negative quality. Notice what Peter commands us immediately after describing the church as holy: "Dearly beloved, I beseech you as strangers and pilgrims, abstain from fleshly lusts, which war against the soul" (1 Pet. 2:11).

Ringgren, and Heinz-Josef Fabry, trans. Douglas W. Stott (Grand Rapids: William B. Eerdmans Publishing Company, 1999), 10:148.

We must be sure we understand the difference between the *world* as the sum of all persons living on planet earth and the *world* as a domain of human existence with a system of values that Satan has crafted to entice people into living outside the will of God.[4] The former meaning of *world* is evident in John 3:16, a well-known verse that declares, "For God so loved the world, that he gave his only begotten Son." John uses the latter meaning of the term when he writes,

> Love not the world, neither the things that are in the world. If any man love the world, the love of the Father is not in him. For all that is in the world, the lust of the flesh, and the lust of the eyes, and the pride of life, is not of the Father, but is of the world. And the world passeth away, and the lust thereof: but he that doeth the will of God abideth forever. (1 John 2:15–17)

These three categories of strong enticement—fleshly, visual, and prideful—were exactly what Satan used in tempting both Eve (Gen. 3:6) and our Savior (Matt. 4:1–11).

Worldliness is a term that describes "an attitude of friendship toward, a desire for, and a wish to be recognized by the world system."[5] Worldliness in a Christian's heart violates the command of 1 John 2:15–17. We must be careful that we do not stereotype

---

[4]Joachim Guhrt describes the *world* in John's writings as "a uniform subject which opposes God in enmity, resists the redeeming work of the Son, does not believe in him, and indeed hates him (7:7; 15:18ff,). It is ruled by the prince of this cosmos (12:31; 16:11), i.e. the Evil One (1 John 5:18)." "κόσμος," *The New International Dictionary of New Testament Theology*, ed. Colin Brown (Grand Rapids: Zondervan Publishing House, 1975), 1:525.

[5]Mark Sidwell, *The Dividing Line: Understanding and Applying Biblical Separation* (Greenville, SC: Bob Jones University Press, 1998), 29. This book is a succinct and accurate presentation of biblical separation.

worldliness because it is foundationally an attitude, not an action. Satan is quite creative in tailoring many different forms of worldliness because people vary widely in their tastes, aspirations, and affections. A form of worldliness that does not appeal to me may ensnare someone else, but I should not congratulate myself that I have not fallen into worldliness simply by avoiding what does not appeal to me!

Perhaps an illustration will aid in understanding the multiform aspects of worldliness. Satan has successfully used a desire for illegal drugs to snare some people with the promise of fleshly enjoyment. Smoking marijuana, snorting cocaine, or shooting heroin has become an addictive lifestyle for millions of people worldwide. I think most Christians would conclude that such a lifestyle is worldly because it reflects a devotion to physical pleasure (the lust of the flesh) above stewardship of the physical body (a recognition of the body's holiness, or devotion to God). I have never been tempted to experiment with drugs. But I must not conclude that I have no problem with worldliness simply because I consider the use of illegal drugs disgusting. Satan knows he can find some form of worldliness that does appeal to me. I have to be on my guard continually so that the devil does not use some aspect of the world system to draw my heart's affection away from Christ and His will. Worldliness can be exceedingly subtle, just as the author of the world system is (Gen. 3:1).

DRINKING ALCOHOL TODAY IS A FORM OF WORLDLINESS

It is necessary at this point in our discussion to consider whether or not the consumption of modern alcoholic beverages falls within the definition of worldliness. We have already seen that people in biblical times consumed highly diluted alcoholic drinks. Even our Savior consumed these beverages as any normal Israelite in that day would (Matt. 11:19). Christ never sinned, so satisfying one's need for variety and well-being with a beverage that people normally used was not worldliness. People in Bible times viewed wine as an agricultural blessing from God's hand, another viable source of hydration. But is that how we still view alcohol today? The answer is a resounding *no*! We commit a serious error when we automatically conclude that there is cultural continuity between the biblical setting and our modern period. Due to the vast differences in both the alcoholic content of ancient drinks and the reasons people drank them, we must not assume that what was acceptable in biblical days is automatically acceptable today.

The devil has been very clever in getting Christians today to view the consumption of alcoholic beverages as something that Christ would do if He were living in our society. When a preacher today takes his stand for abstinence, some will charge him with establishing a standard that is holier than our Savior would adopt! This sort of charge is a result of the devil's strategy. Paul admonished the believers at Corinth to be careful "lest Satan should get an advantage of us; for we are not ignorant of his devices" (2 Cor. 2:11).

Satan has established the consumption of alcoholic beverages today as an important aspect of unsaved culture. Sophisticated drinkers seek the experience of collecting and consuming only the very best wines, often expending hundreds or even thousands of dollars on one bottle of a superior vintage. Alcohol has become by far the most widely abused drug in America. For the experience of temporarily forgetting how meaningless and empty their lives are, millions of unsaved people risk their health, marriages, children, jobs, and even their own lives by drinking. Drinking is an easy escape from reality. My four years of association with hard-drinking engineering colleagues in the paper industry convinced me that alcohol consumption was not a peripheral activity in their lives— it was central. The people I knew drank because only inebriation brought a few hours of relief from the misery of their dull, boring lives. So the broad spectrum of those who drink, all the way from the sophisticated connoisseur of wine to the undiscriminating bum in the gutter, is united by the desire to have some experience that satisfies human pride or lust. Why would a Christian want *any* association with such a lifestyle? Given the biblical and cultural realities of alcohol consumption, an interpreter must conclude that if Christ were living among us in our day, He would stay away entirely from the consumption of alcohol because drinking has become an integral part of the world system that Satan has crafted to destroy human lives.

Drinking alcoholic beverages is also a means by which worldly people know who shares their worldview. There is camaraderie and acceptance around the shared experience of drinking. One time when I was in a management meeting of employees from a major paper company, I heard an executive assure the group that he would never trust anyone who would not get drunk with him. For this fellow, drinking was an experience that had become a bond of solidarity among those who were committed to worldly culture. Worldly people know how incongruous it is for a Christian to verbalize a testimony of salvation and then join in with the crowd consuming alcoholic beverages.

A student of mine recently wrote out his testimony of salvation, including his description of deliverance from the lifestyle of drinking. He was working for a car dealership when he came to know the Lord. He asked the Lord to take away his desire for alcohol, and God answered his prayer by making even the smell of it repugnant to him. He had only one subsequent encounter with drinking:

> I had no desire to drink until the dealership had a charity golf tournament. At that tournament a few of the employees and participants ordered a Bloody Mary, an alcoholic drink consisting of vodka and tomato juice. I did not see the harm in having one, so I too ordered the same drink. As I was consuming my beverage, a gentleman to whom I had professed my Christianity approached me and asked if I were drinking a Bloody Mary. After I answered affirmatively, he made a statement that struck conviction into my heart. He said, "I didn't know Christians drank." I looked at my drink, which I had only partially consumed, and threw it out saying, "You are right, we don't drink." I asked his forgiveness as well as God's and will look back on that day realizing that even some unsaved people know what is right and wrong before a holy God.

But some Christians are naive enough to think that the consumption of alcoholic beverages is simply a matter of personal Christian conscience—one of those "gray areas" that the Bible really does not address.

We must realize that *everything we do as believers* demonstrates whether we are sojourners in this present evil age or those who are seeking to find fulfillment in what the world system has to offer. It is vitally important that unsaved people who are watching our lives see evidence of the holiness that marks the transformed character and actions of those who profess to know Jesus Christ. *Repudiation of alcohol is not legalism*—it is living out the gospel in daily life. Sanctification demands a lifestyle that does not pander to worldly acceptance or desires. The avoidance of alcohol is one of the clearest outward behaviors signaling a distinctive difference in a Christian's lifestyle. We ought to use such clarity as an opportunity to present the good news of salvation in Christ to everyone who asks why we refuse to identify with Satan's world system.

We must also guard our testimony with other believers. I may not even know, for example, that someone in the church I attend used to be an alcoholic before he or she was saved. I would not want to defile my conscience by knowing I did something that encouraged a fellow Christian to fall back into addiction to alcohol. As we saw in Chapter 1, Paul addressed this issue of living in a way that would not cause a fellow believer to fall into sin. In the context of 1 Corinthians 8:10–13, Paul was dealing with the issue of whether or not a Christian should eat meat at the venue of an idol's temple. The overall principle he states is just as applicable to the issue of drinking alcohol. When Paul states the same principle in Romans 14:21, he also includes the practice of drinking wine: "It is good neither to eat flesh, nor to drink wine, nor anything whereby thy brother stumbleth, or is offended, or is made weak." A Christian should want his life to be an example of devotion to Christ, not a model of how to flirt with the world system.

The example a believer sets in the home is even more important than his testimony in the church or society at large. Children are highly impressionable, and what they see a parent do at home they are prone to take even further in their own lives. Our Savior asserted the importance of providing children with a good example: "And whoso shall receive one such little child in my name receiveth me. But whoso shall offend [i.e., cause to stumble into sin] one of these little ones which believe in me, it were better for him that a millstone were hanged about his neck, and that he were drowned in the depth of the sea" (Matt. 18:5–6). I cannot even begin to imagine the grief of heart a parent would experience by realizing that the example he or she had set by consuming alcoholic beverages in the home influenced a child to drink later in life, leading to tragic results.

CONCLUSION

The beverage use of alcohol is incompatible with growth in personal holiness. A believer who drinks is setting a disastrous example for fellow Christians and the children who grow up in his own home. There is no continuity between what ancient people drank and what modern people consume.[6] We have plenty of nonalcoholic options from which to choose. Norman L. Geisler notes that "people in the United States have plenty of wholesome, nonaddictive beverages. The situation today is unlike biblical times when there were not many wholesome beverages."[7] We ought to be growing in holiness and not cozying up to the world system. Let's be careful to set the biblical standard correctly for the generations that follow us. "Whether therefore ye eat, or drink, or whatsoever ye do, do all to the glory of God" (1 Cor. 10:31).

Perhaps it would be helpful to the reader if I review in succinct fashion the arguments I have made through the course of establishing my position of abstaining from the use of alcoholic beverages:

---

[6]As mentioned in Chapters 1 and 3, Robert H. Stein shows that the wine in biblical times was routinely diluted with water. (See "Is New Testament 'Wine' the Same as Today's Wine?" in *Difficult Passages in the New Testament*.) Peter Masters likewise asserts, "The normal beverage wine of Palestine in those days was very much weaker than the table wines, fortified wines and spirits of later ages, and there was no risk whatsoever of alcohol-dependency or alcoholism being triggered unless a drinker went a very long way beyond the ordinary levels of consumption." *Should Christians Drink? The Case for Total Abstinence* (London: Wakeman Trust, 1992), 80.

[7]Norman Giesler, "A Christian Perspective on Wine-Drinking," *Bibliotheca Sacra* 139 (January–March, 1982): 53. This article is an excellent defense of abstinence from alcoholic beverages.

- Drinking today has produced incredibly disastrous effects in our society. Crime, disease, and death are closely connected with alcohol use. A Christian should have no association with something that has blighted and destroyed lives as alcohol has.

- There is no legitimate correspondence between what people in biblical days consumed and the highly intoxicating beverages people drink today.

- The argument one sometimes hears, "Jesus drank wine, so I can too," is unfounded. He drank the highly diluted wine of the normal Israelite, not the outrageously intoxicating alcoholic beverages of our day. If Christ lived among us today, He would have no part in consuming alcohol.

- The New Testament demands that the Christian lovingly embrace only what edifies himself and others. The Scripture also requires that we repudiate anything that might potentially enslave us. Alcohol use does absolutely nothing to edify anyone, and it risks a devastating enslavement.

- The Bible warns us in Proverbs 23:31 about the use of undiluted wine. Drinking modern wine, therefore, is a clear violation of a scriptural prohibition. Many other scriptural passages warn about potential abuse of the diluted wine that ancient people normally consumed. If diluted wine could be abused, then such warnings are far more alarming in relation to modern alcoholic drinks. Modern believers, therefore, ought to completely shun the use of alcohol.

- There is a genetic propensity for alcohol abuse in some people, and no one knows whether or not he is more susceptible to alcoholism. Alcohol is also a mind-altering substance. Only through total abstinence can a person ensure that he will never become a drunk. Drinking is like playing Russian roulette with a real gun loaded with real bullets. We are stewards of the bodies that God has given to us, and no steward ought to act in such a cavalier manner.

• Consumption of alcoholic beverages for achieving health benefits is both unnecessary and dangerous. Exercise, proper nutrition, and supervision by medical professionals are legitimate pathways to proper stewardship of the body for the Christian.

• Drinking is a terrible example to others, both saved and lost. The New Testament demands that we live in a way that does not cause others to stumble into sin. The example we set, especially for our own children, must include total abstinence from alcohol.

• Drinking today is a form of worldliness. It is a sin for a Christian to love the world system (1 John 2:15–17). We ought to instead be growing in holiness.

APPENDIX 1:
OCCURRENCES OF THE HEBREW WORD *YĀYĬN*

Reference	Contextual Indications of Meaning
Gen. 9:21	Noah drinks *yāyĭn* and becomes drunk.
Gen. 9:24	Noah awakens from his *yāyĭn* (he was very inebriated).
Gen. 14:18	Melchizedek brings Abraham bread and *yāyĭn* to sustain him.
Gen. 19:32	Lot's daughters plan to make him drink *yāyĭn* so they can have incestuous relations with him.
Gen. 19:33	Lot becomes drunk with *yāyĭn*, and the elder daughter has intercourse with him.
Gen. 19:34	The next night the younger daughter decides on the same plan.
Gen. 19:35	Lot is so drunk with *yāyĭn* that he has intercourse with his younger daughter.
Gen. 27:25	Jacob brings Isaac meat to eat and *yāyĭn* to drink so that his father would bless him.
Gen. 49:11	Jacob blesses Judah with the prophecy that Judah will wash his garments in *yāyĭn* and his clothes in the "blood of grapes."
Gen. 49:12	The blessing continues: Judah's eyes will be sparkling from *yāyĭn* and his teeth white from milk.
Exod. 29:40	A quarter of a hin of *yāyĭn* was to be a drink offering.
Lev. 10:9	Priests must not drink *yāyĭn* or strong drink when they serve in the tabernacle.
Lev. 23:13	A quarter of a hin of *yāyĭn* was to be a drink offering.
Num. 6:3	The person who takes the vow of a Nazirite must abstain from *yāyĭn*, strong drink, grape juice, and raisins.
Num. 6:4	As long as a person is under the vow of a Nazirite, he/she must not eat anything that is made from the grape vine [lit. "the vine of the *yāyĭn*"].
Num. 6:20	After the Nazirite is released from his vow, he may drink *yāyĭn*.
Num. 15:5	A quarter of a hin of *yāyĭn* was to be a drink offering.
Num. 15:10	A half of a hin of *yāyĭn* was to be a drink offering.
Num. 28:14	A half of a hin of *yāyĭn* was to be a drink offering.
Deut. 14:26	An Israelite could spend his money for whatever his heart desired: oxen, sheep, *yāyĭn*, or strong drink. Then he would consume it in the Lord's presence and rejoice.
Deut. 28:39	When God's judgment falls, Israelites will plant vineyards but not drink any *yāyĭn* because worms will destroy the grapes.

Deut. 29:5 (6)	Because God supplied all of Israel's needs in the wilderness, they have not eaten bread or drunk *yăyĭn* or strong drink.
Deut. 32:33	Because it comes from the grapes of Sodom and Gomorrah, Israel's *yăyĭn* is the venom of serpents.
Deut. 32:38	Israel offers drink offerings of *yăyĭn* to false gods.
Josh. 9:4	The crafty Gibeonites use worn-out "skins of *yăyĭn*."
Josh. 9:13	Gibeonites lie about the age of their "skins of *yăyĭn*."
Judg. 13:4	The Angel of Yahweh commands Samson's mother not to drink *yăyĭn* or strong drink.
Judg. 13:7	Samson's mother repeats the Angel's words to her husband.
Judg. 13:14	The Angel repeats the instructions to Samson's father.
Judg. 19:19	The Levite has everything he needs: straw and fodder for the donkeys, and bread and *yăyĭn* for himself.
1 Sam. 1:14	Eli remonstrates with Hannah for being drunk and tells her to put away her *yăyĭn*.
1 Sam. 1:15	Hannah says that she has consumed neither *yăyĭn* nor strong drink—she is simply oppressed in spirit.
1 Sam. 1:24	Hannah takes Samuel to Shiloh with food and a jug of *yăyĭn*.
1 Sam. 10:3	Samuel tells Saul he will meet three men, and one will have a jug of *yăyĭn*.
1 Sam. 16:20	Jesse loads a donkey with bread, a jug of *yăyĭn*, and a young goat for David to take as a gift for Saul.
1 Sam. 25:18	Abigail takes provisions to David: two hundred loaves of bread, two jugs of *yăyĭn*, five sheep, five measures of roasted grain, one hundred clusters of raisins, and two hundred fig cakes.
1 Sam. 25:37	Nabal becomes sober when the *yăyĭn* goes out of him.
2 Sam. 13:28	Amnon's drunken state is described as his heart being "merry with *yăyĭn*."
2 Sam. 16:1	Ziba meets David with provisions: two hundred loaves of bread, one hundred clusters of raisins, one hundred summer fruits, and a jug of *yăyĭn*.
2 Sam. 16:2	The *yăyĭn* is for "whoever is faint in the wilderness."
1 Chron. 9:29	Levitical guards are appointed over items associated with worship, including *yăyĭn*.
1 Chron. 12:41 (40)	During the celebration of David's coronation, people bring provisions in great quantities: flour cakes, fig cakes, bunches of raisins, *yăyĭn*, oil, oxen, and sheep.
1 Chron. 27:27	David's assets include storehouses of *yăyĭn*.
2 Chron. 2:9 (10)	Solomon pays Hiram for the workers and timber he provided for the temple. The payment includes twenty thousand baths of *yăyĭn*.
2 Chron. 2:14 (15)	Hiram accepts the payment of *yăyĭn* and other commodities.
2 Chron. 11:11	Solomon strengthens his fortress and puts in stores of food, oil, and *yăyĭn*.
Neh. 2:1	Nehemiah takes *yăyĭn* and gives it to the king.

Neh. 5:15	Nehemiah is not like the former governors who took bread, *yăyĭn*, and silver from the people.
Neh. 5:18	Nehemiah's daily living allowance consists of one ox, six sheep, birds, and all kinds of *yăyĭn*.
Neh. 13:15	Some people are violating the Sabbath by treading *yăyĭn* presses.
Esther 1:7	Royal *yăyĭn* is plentiful according to the king's bounty.
Esther 1:10	When the king is drunk, his heart is "merry with *yăyĭn*."
Esther 5:6	People drink their *yăyĭn* at the banquet.
Esther 7:2	People drink *yăyĭn* on the second day of the banquet.
Esther 7:7	The king arises in his anger from drinking *yăyĭn*.
Esther 7:8	The king returns to the place where people were drinking *yăyĭn*.
Job 1:13	Job's children are eating and drinking *yăyĭn*.
Job 1:18	Disaster falls as Job's children are eating and drinking *yăyĭn*.
Job 32:19	Job's belly is like unvented *yăyĭn*, like new wineskins about to burst.
Ps. 60:5 (3)	In judgment God gives His people "*yăyĭn* of staggering."
Ps. 75:9 (8)	In judgment God gives the wicked *yăyĭn* to drink that He has mixed.
Ps. 78:65	The Lord awakes like a warrior who was overcome by *yăyĭn*.
Ps. 104:15	*Yăyĭn* makes man's heart glad, oil makes his face glisten, and food sustains his heart.
Prov. 4:17	Evil men eat the bread of wickedness and drink the *yăyĭn* of violence.
Prov. 9:2	Wisdom has prepared her meat and mixed her *yăyĭn*.
Prov. 9:5	Wisdom bids people to eat her food and drink the *yăyĭn* she has mixed.
Prov. 20:1	*Yăyĭn* is a mocker, strong drink a brawler, and whoever is going astray/staggering in it is not wise.
Prov. 21:17	He who is loving pleasure will become poor, and he who is loving *yăyĭn* and oil will not become rich.
Prov. 23:20	Do not be with heavy drinkers of *yăyĭn* or with gluttons.
Prov. 23:30	Those who linger long over *yăyĭn* and go to investigate mixed wine will have disastrous problems.
Prov. 23:31	Do not look on the *yăyĭn* when it is red, when it "giveth his colour in the cup, when it moveth itself aright."
Prov. 31:4	Kings should not drink *yăyĭn* or desire strong drink.
Prov. 31:6	Give strong drink to the person who is perishing and *yăyĭn* to the one whose life is bitter.
Eccles. 2:3	Solomon seeks to stimulate his body with *yăyĭn* while his mind is guiding him wisely.
Eccles. 9:7	Eat bread in happiness and drink *yăyĭn* with a cheerful heart.
Eccles. 10:19	People make bread for laughter, *yăyĭn* makes life merry, and money is the answer to all.
Song of Sol. 1:2	Your love is better than *yăyĭn*.

Song of Sol. 1:4	We will extol your love more than *yăyĭn*.
Song of Sol. 2:4	He brings me to the "house of *yăyĭn*," and his banner over me is love.
Song of Sol. 4:10	How much better is your love than *yăyĭn*.
Song of Sol. 5:1	I have drunk my *yăyĭn* and my milk.
Song of Sol. 7:9 (10)	Your mouth is like the best *yăyĭn*.
Song of Sol. 8:2	I will give you spiced *yăyĭn* to drink from the juice of my pomegranates.
Isa. 5:11	Woe is pronounced on those who arise early to pursue strong drink and stay up late until *yăyĭn* inflames them.
Isa. 5:12	All sorts of musical instruments and *yăyĭn* are in their feasts.
Isa. 5:22	Woe is pronounced on those who are heroes in drinking *yăyĭn* and men of capacity in mixing strong drink.
Isa. 16:10	In the vineyards no one rejoices; no one treads in the *yăyĭn* presses.
Isa. 22:13	Instead of mourning over impending judgment, there is gaiety and gladness, killing of animals to eat, and drinking of *yăyĭn*.
Isa. 24:9	In God's judgment people will not drink *yăyĭn* with a song, and strong drink will be bitter to those who consume it.
Isa. 24:11	There is an outcry because the *yăyĭn* is all gone, and all joy turns to gloom.
Isa. 28:1	Woe to the drunkards of Ephraim who are struck with *yăyĭn*.
Isa. 28:7	Even Judah's leaders, priests and prophets, reel with *yăyĭn* and stagger from strong drink.
Isa. 29:9	God will cause a supernatural blindness in His people that is not the result of physical intoxication from *yăyĭn* or strong drink.
Isa. 51:21	God will remedy the condition of His afflicted people who have been drunk—but not with *yăyĭn*. His judgment will fall on Judah's enemies.
Isa. 55:1	God compares His free offer of salvation to obtaining life-giving hydration: water, *yăyĭn*, and milk.
Isa. 56:12	The shepherds of God's people are derelict in their duties and addicted to *yăyĭn* and strong drink.
Jer. 13:12	God's judgment is pictured as every jug being full of *yăyĭn*.
Jer. 23:9	Jeremiah's heart is so broken over the false prophets who have led Israel astray that He has become like a man overcome with *yăyĭn*.
Jer. 25:15	The Lord tells Jeremiah to take a cup from His hand filled with the *yăyĭn* of His wrath and to make all the nations drink from it.
Jer. 35:2	The Lord tells Jeremiah to give *yăyĭn* to the Rechabites.
Jer. 35:5	Jeremiah sets bowls full of *yăyĭn* and some cups before the Rechabites and tells them to drink it.
Jer. 35:6	The Rechabites refuse to drink the *yăyĭn*.
Jer. 35:8	The Rechabites assert that they have obeyed their ancestor Jonadab in refusing to drink *yăyĭn*.

Jer. 35:14	Although the Rechabites have obeyed Jonadab's command not to drink *yăyĭn*, God's people have not obeyed His commands.
Jer. 40:10	Gedaliah commands the remnant of people left in Judah to gather in *yăyĭn*, summer fruit, and oil.
Jer. 40:12	The people of Judah gather in *yăyĭn* and summer fruit abundantly.
Jer. 48:33	God takes joy and gladness away from Moab by making *yăyĭn* cease from the wine presses.
Jer. 51:7	Babylon is a golden cup in the Lord's hand intoxicating all the earth with her *yăyĭn*.
Lam. 2:12	Children die on the streets of the city as they ask their mothers, "Where is grain and *yăyĭn*?"
Ezek. 27:18	*Yăyĭn* is listed as one type of wealth along with wool, wrought iron, cassia, and sweet cane.
Ezek. 44:21	In the future temple the priests must not drink *yăyĭn* when they enter the inner court.
Dan. 1:5	The king appoints a daily ration for the young Jewish exiles from his choice food and from the *yăyĭn* he drank.
Dan. 1:8	Daniel made up his mind that he would not defile himself with either the king's food or his *yăyĭn*.
Dan. 1:16	The king's overseer keeps giving Daniel and his colleagues vegetables instead of the king's food and *yăyĭn*.
Dan. 10:3	Daniel fasted for three weeks; no meat or *yăyĭn* entered his mouth.
Hosea 4:11	Harlotry, *yăyĭn*, and new wine "take away the heart."
Hosea 7:5	Princes become sick with the heat of *yăyĭn*.
Hosea 9:4	When God judges His people, there will be no more *yăyĭn* to use as a drink offering or bread to satisfy their hunger.
Hosea 14:8 (7)	When God turns His people from their apostasy, they will be famous like the *yăyĭn* of Lebanon.
Joel 1:5	Drunkards are aroused from sleep to weep—all who are drinkers of *yăyĭn* and sweet wine.
Joel 4:3 (3:3)	God will judge the nations at the Valley of Jehoshaphat because they have sold a girl so that they may drink *yăyĭn*.
Amos 2:8	God will punish Israel because they drink the *yăyĭn* of those who have been fined.
Amos 2:12	God's people make Nazirites drink *yăyĭn*.
Amos 5:11	God's judgment prevents sinners from drinking the *yăyĭn* that their vineyards produce.
Amos 6:6	God's judgment falls on people living in luxury, those who drink *yăyĭn* from bowls used in the rituals of sacrifice.
Amos 9:14	In restored Israel, people will plant vineyards and drink their *yăyĭn*.
Mic. 2:11	False prophets pander to prosperous people by promising them plenty of *yăyĭn* and strong drink.

Mic. 6:15	When God's judgment falls, people will do the work of treading grapes but will not drink *yăyĭn*.
Hab. 2:5	*Yăyĭn* betrays the arrogant man.
Zeph. 1:13	People will not drink *yăyĭn* from the vineyards they plant.
Hag. 2:12	If holy meat comes into contact with other food or *yăyĭn*, no transfer of holiness occurs.
Zech. 9:15	When God protects His people, they will drink and be boisterous as with *yăyĭn*.
Zech. 10:7	When God restores Ephraim, their heart will rejoice—as if from *yăyĭn*.

APPENDIX 2:
USES OF THE HEBREW WORD *TÎRÔŠ*

Reference	Contextual Indications of Meaning
Gen. 27:28	Isaac blesses Jacob with the dew of heaven, fatness of the earth, and plenty of grain and *tîrôš*.
Gen. 27:37	Isaac tells Esau he has blessed Jacob with sovereignty over his brothers, and with grain and *tîrôš*.
Num. 18:12	Priests get the best of the oil, *tîrôš*, grain, and first fruits that are given to the Lord.
Deut. 7:13	If Israel keeps the covenant, God will give them many children, grain, *tîrôš*, and increase of livestock.
Deut. 11:14	God will give rain that will produce grain, *tîrôš*, and oil.
Deut. 12:17	Israelites are not allowed to eat the tithe in their cities: grain, *tîrôš*, oil, or firstborn of animals.
Deut. 14:23	Israelites should eat the tithe at the designated place: grain, *tîrôš*, oil, and firstborn animals.
Deut. 18:4	The priest should get the first fruits of grain, *tîrôš*, oil, and the first shearing of the sheep.
Deut. 28:51	A foreign nation will devour Israel's grain, *tîrôš*, oil, and increase of the herd and flock.
Deut. 33:28	Israel dwells securely in a land of grain, *tîrôš*, and dew from heaven.
Judg. 9:13	In Jotham's parable, the vine asks if it should stop making *tîrôš*, which cheers God and men.
2 Kings 18:32	The Rabshakeh offers Judeans a productive land of grain and *tîrôš*, bread and vineyards, olive trees and honey.
2 Chron. 31:5	Israelites bring tithes of grain, *tîrôš*, oil, honey, and produce of the field.
2 Chron. 32:28	Hezekiah had storehouses for grain, *tîrôš*, and oil.
Neh. 5:11	Unfair nobles and rulers are to give back the grain, *tîrôš*, and oil they took from the people.
Neh. 10:37 (38)	Returned captives will bring the tithe of meal, fruit of every tree, *tîrôš*, and oil.
Neh. 10:39 (40)	Israelites bring the tithes into the temple: grain, *tîrôš*, and oil.
Neh. 13:5	A large room in the temple stored the tithes of grain, *tîrôš*, and oil.
Neh. 13:12	Judah brought into the storehouse the tithes of grain, *tîrôš*, and oil.
Ps. 4:7 (8)	God has put more gladness in the heart than when grain and *tîrôš* abound.
Prov. 3:10	Barns will be filled, and vats will overflow with *tîrôš*.
Isa. 24:7	God's curse causes *tîrôš* to mourn and the vine to decay; all revelry ceases.

Isa. 36:17	The Rabshakeh promises a land of grain and *tîrôš*, a land of bread and vineyards.
Isa. 62:8	The Lord will never again give Jerusalem's grain to feed her enemies or her *tîrôš* for foreign people.
Isa. 65:8	As *tîrôš* is found in the cluster of grapes, so there is yet blessing in Judah.
Jer. 31:12	God's goodness will again produce grain, *tîrôš*, and oil.
Hosea 2:8 (10)	God gives His people grain, *tîrôš*, and oil.
Hosea 2:9 (11)	Because Israel used God's benefits to worship Baal, He will take back His grain and *tîrôš* in its season.
Hosea 2:22 (24)	The earth will respond to the grain, *tîrôš*, and oil.
Hosea 4:11	Harlotry, wine, and *tîrôš* take away the heart [functions of the intellect, emotion, and will].
Hosea 7:14	Rebellious Israel wants only grain and *tîrôš*.
Hosea 9:2	Israel is spiritually adulterous, so God will cause the threshing floor, the wine vat, and the *tîrôš* to fail.
Joel 1:10	God's judgment causes the destruction of grain, *tîrôš*, and oil.
Joel 2:19	When God has pity on His people, He will send grain, *tîrôš*, and oil.
Joel 2:24	God promises that once again the threshing floors will be full of grain and the vats will overflow with *tîrôš* and oil.
Mic. 6:15	When God's judgment falls, the people will sow but not reap, tread olives but not anoint themselves, and tread grapes but not drink the *tîrôš*.
Hag. 1:11	The land will withhold its produce: grain, *tîrôš*, and oil.
Zech. 9:17	God will bless His people: grain will make the young men flourish, and *tîrôš* the young women.

APPENDIX 3:
USES OF THE HEBREW WORD 'ĀSÎS

Reference	Contextual Indications of Meaning
Song of Sol. 8:2	Here 'āsîs does not refer to a grape product, but to the juice of a pomegranate.
Isa. 49:26	Israel's oppressors will be drunk with their own blood as with 'āsîs.
Joel 1:5	Drunkards will lament because they have no more 'āsîs to drink.
Joel 3:18 (4:18)	In the future kingdom the mountains will drip with 'āsîs, and the hills will flow with milk.
Amos 9:13	In the future kingdom the mountains and the hills will drip 'āsîs.

APPENDIX 4:
USES OF THE HEBREW WORD *ŠĒKĀR*

Reference	Contextual Indications of Meaning
Lev. 10:9	Priests are forbidden to drink wine or *šēkār* when serving in the tabernacle.
Num. 6:3	The Nazirite must not drink wine or *šēkār*.
Num. 6:3	The Nazirite must not drink vinegar made from *šēkār*.
Num. 28:7	The drink offering of *šēkār* must be poured out in the holy place.
Deut. 14:26	An Israelite is to drink wine or *šēkār* in the Lord's presence.
Deut. 29:6 (5)	During the forty-year wilderness wandering, the Israelites drink neither wine nor *šēkār*.
Judg. 13:4	The Angel of Yahweh appears to Samson's mother and tells her she must not drink wine or *šēkār*.
Judg. 13:7	Samson's mother tells her husband that she must not drink wine or *šēkār*.
Judg. 13:14	The Angel tells Manoah that Samson's mother must not drink wine or *šēkār*.
1 Sam. 1:15	Hannah tells Eli that she is not drunk; she has consumed no wine or *šēkār*.
Ps. 69:12 (13)	The psalmist complains that he is the subject of the song of those who are drinking *šēkār*.
Prov. 20:1	Wine is a mocker, and *šēkār* is a brawler.
Prov. 31:4	Kings should not drink wine nor princes *šēkār*.
Prov. 31:6	Give *šēkār* to the person who is perishing.
Isa. 5:11	Woe to those who arise early to pursue *šēkār*.
Isa. 5:22	Woe to those who are valiant in mixing *šēkār*.
Isa. 24:9	When God's judgment falls, *šēkār* will be bitter to those who drink it.
Isa. 28:7	The drunkards of Ephraim stagger from *šēkār*.
Isa. 28:7	The priest and the prophet reel with *šēkār*.
Isa. 28:7	They stagger from *šēkār*.
Isa. 29:9	God's judgment, not *šēkār*, has made people stagger.
Isa. 56:12	Israel's watchmen drink heavily of *šēkār*.
Mic. 2:11	Israel deserves lying prophets who promise plenty of wine and *šēkār*.

Appendix 5:
Uses of the Greek Word *Oinos*

Reference	Contextual Indications of Meaning
Matt. 9:17	People do not put new *oinos* into old wineskins.
Matt. 9:17	The *oinos* pours out of wineskins that have burst.
Matt. 9:17	So people put new *oinos* into new wineskins, and both are preserved.
Matt. 27:34	Christ on the cross refuses to drink *oinos* (KJV "vinegar").
Mark 2:22	No one puts new *oinos* into old wineskins.
Mark 2:22	Otherwise the *oinos* will burst the wineskin.
Mark 2:22	Then both the *oinos* and the wineskins are lost.
Mark 2:22	So new *oinos* is put into new wineskins.
Mark 15:23	Christ on the cross refuses to drink *oinos* mixed with myrrh.
Luke 1:15	An angel predicts that John the Baptist will drink no *oinos* or strong drink.
Luke 5:37	No one puts new *oinos* into old wineskins.
Luke 5:37	Otherwise the new *oinos* will burst the wineskins.
Luke 5:38	New *oinos* must be put into new wineskins.
Luke 7:33	John the Baptist has neither eaten bread nor consumed *oinos*, and people conclude he has a demon.
Luke 10:34	The good Samaritan pours oil and *oinos* into the injured man's wounds.
John 2:3	The *oinos* at the wedding feast runs out.
John 2:3	Mary tells Jesus, "They have no *oinos*."
John 2:9	When the ruler of the feast tastes the water that has been made *oinos*, he does not know its origin.
John 2:10	The ruler of the feast tells the bridegroom that normally people serve the good *oinos* first.
John 2:10	The ruler of the feast does not understand why the bridegroom has kept the best *oinos* until after the guests have drunk freely.
John 4:46	Jesus comes again to Cana where He made the water *oinos*.
Rom. 14:21	Paul commends not eating meat, drinking *oinos*, or doing anything that causes a brother to stumble.
Eph. 5:18	Paul commands believers not to get drunk with *oinos*.
1 Tim. 3:8	Deacons must not be "given to much *oinos*."
1 Tim. 5:23	Paul commands Timothy to "use a little *oinos*" for the sake of his stomach and his frequent ailments.
Titus 2:3	Older women must not be enslaved to much *oinos*.

Rev. 6:6	As the third seal is broken, John hears a voice say, "See thou hurt not the oil and the *oinos*."
Rev. 14:8	Babylon makes all the nations drink "of the *oinos* of the wrath of her fornication."
Rev. 14:10	Those who worship the beast will "drink of the *oinos* of the wrath of God" full strength.
Rev. 16:19	God gives Babylon "the cup of the *oinos* of the fierceness of his wrath."
Rev. 17:2	"The inhabitants of the earth have been made drunk with the *oinos*" of Babylon's fornication.
Rev. 18:3	"All the nations have drunk of the *oinos* of the wrath" of Babylon's fornication.
Rev. 18:13	*Oinos* is listed along with twenty-seven other commodities in 18:12–13 that the kings of the earth can no longer procure from Babylon.
Rev. 19:15	At His Second Coming, Christ treads the winepress of the *oinos* of God's fierce wrath.

References Cited

Akin, Daniel L. "The Emerging Church and Ethical Choices: the Corinthian Matrix," in *Evangelicals Engaging Emergent: A Discussion of the Emergent Church Movement*, edited by William D. Henard and Adam W. Greenway, 262–80. Nashville: B & H Publishing Group, 2009.

Alexander, Joseph Addison. *The Psalms: Translated and Explained.* 1873. Reprint, Grand Rapids: Baker Book House, 1975.

Amerine, Maynard A. "Wine," in *Collier's Encyclopedia*, edited by Lauren S. Bahr, 23:517–21. New York: P. F. Collier, 1996.

Archer, Gleason L., Jr. *A Survey of Old Testament Introduction, Revised and Expanded.* Chicago: Moody Publishers, 2007.

Arndt, W. F., and Gingrich, F. W. *A Greek-English Lexicon of the New Testament and Other Early Christian Literature.* Chicago: University of Chicago Press, 1957.

Arnst, Catherine. "Can Alcoholism Be Treated?" *Business Week,* April 11, 2005, 96–97.

Athanaeus. *The Deipnosophists*, translated by Charles Burton Gulick, in Loeb Classical Library, edited by T. E. Page. Cambridge, MA: Harvard University Press, 1961.

Bandstra, Barry L. "Wine Press, Winevat," in *International Standard Bible Encyclopedia*, 4:1072. Grand Rapids: William B. Eerdmans Publishing Company, 1988.

Barnes, Albert. *Notes on the New Testament.* 1885. Reprint, Grand Rapids: Baker Book House, 1956.

Barrett, Stephen. "Resveratrol: Don't Buy the Hype." Accessed October 21, 2013. http://quackwatch.com/01QuackeryRelatedTopics/DSH/resveratrol.html.

Böhmer, Heinrich. *Luther in Light of Recent Research*, translated by Carl F. Huth Jr. New York: Christian Herald, 1916.

Bouwsma, William J. *John Calvin: A Sixteenth-Century Portrait.* London: Oxford University Press, 1988.

Brink, Susan. "Your Brain on Alcohol." *U.S. News & World Report*, April 29, 2001, http://www.usnews.com/usnews/culture/articles/010507/archive_001356_2.htm.

Brown University Center for Alcohol and Addiction Studies. "Position Paper on Drug Policy: Physician Leadership on National Drug Policy (PLNDP)," 2000. Accessed October 28, 2013. http://www.plndp.org /Resources/researchrpt.pdf.

Brown, Colin. "Vine, Wine," in *New International Dictionary of New Testament Theology*, edited by Colin Brown. 3:921. Grand Rapids: Zondervan Publishing House, 1978.

Brown, Francis, S. R. Driver, and Charles A. Briggs. *A Hebrew and English Lexicon of the Old Testament.* Oxford: Oxford University Press, 1975

Bustanoby, Andre S. *The Wrath of Grapes: Drinking and the Church Divided.* Grand Rapids: Baker Book House, 1987.

Carpenter, Eugene. "יַיִן," in *New International Dictionary of Old Testament Theology and Exegesis*, edited by Willem A. VanGemeren. 2:375–76. Grand Rapids: Zondervan Publishing House, 1997.

———. "עָסִיס," in *New International Dictionary of Old Testament Theology and Exegesis*, edited by Willem A. VanGemeren. 3:470. Grand Rapids: Zondervan Publishing House, 1997.

Carrao, G., L. Rubbiati, A. Zambon, and C. La Vecchia. "A Meta-analysis of Alcohol Consumption and the Risk of 15 Diseases." *American Journal of Preventive Medicine* 38 (2004): 613–19.

Centers for Disease Control. "Alcohol and Drug Use." Accessed September 2, 2009. http://www.cdc.gov/healthyYouth/alcoholdrug/index.htm.

———. "Quick Stats: General Information on Alcohol Use and Health." Accessed June 14, 2010, http://www.cdc.gov/alcohol/quickstats /general_info.htm.

Cyprian. *The Epistles of S. Cyprian*, Library of Fathers of the Holy Catholic Church, Anterior to the Division of the East and West, trans. by members of the English Church. London: John Henry Parker, 1844.

Daniels, Bruce C. *Puritans at Play: Leisure and Recreation in Colonial America.* New York: St. Martin's Press, 1995.

Dayagi-Mendels, Michal. *Drink and Be Merry: Wine and Beer in Ancient Times.* Jerusalem: The Israel Museum, 1999.

Dommershausen, W. "יַיִן," in *Theological Dictionary of the Old Testament*, edited by G. Johannes Botterweck and Helmer Ringgren, translated by David E. Green. 6:59–64. Grand Rapids: William B. Eerdmans Publishing Company, 1990.

Drummond, Lewis A. *Spurgeon: Prince of Preachers.* Grand Rapids: Kregel Publications, 1992.

Earle, Ralph. *1 Timothy*, Expositor's Bible Commentary, edited by Frank E. Gaebelein. Grand Rapids: Zondervan Publishing House, 1978.

The Evangelical Repository: A Quarterly Magazine of Theological Literature.
Review of *The Wines of the Bible: An Examination and Refutation of the
Unfermented Wine Theory* by A. M. Wilson.1877, vol. 3 (6th series),
307–8.

Fuhs, H. F. "רָאָה," in *Theological Dictionary of the Old Testament*, edited by G
Johannes Botterweck, Helmer Ringgren, and Heinz-Josef Fabry. 13:208–
42. Grand Rapids: William B. Eerdmans Publishing Company, 2004.

Geisler, Norman L. "A Christian Perspective on Wine-Drinking," *Bibliotheca
Sacra* 139 (January–March, 1982): 46–56.

Gentry, Kenneth L. *God Gave Wine: What the Bible Says About Alcohol.*
Lincoln, CA: Oakdown, 2001.

Guhrt, Joachim. "κόσμος," in *New International Dictionary of New Testament
Theology*, edited by Colin Brown. 1:525. Grand Rapids: Zondervan
Publishing House, 1975.

Hamilton, Victor P. *The Book of Genesis: Chapters 1–17*, New International
Commentary on the Old Testament, edited by R. K. Harrison and Robert
L. Hubbard Jr. Grand Rapids: William B. Eerdmans Publishing Company,
1990.

———. *The Book of Genesis, Chapters 18–50*, New International Commentary
on the Old Testament, edited by R K. Harrison and Robert L. Hubbard
Jr. Grand Rapids: William B. Eerdmans Publishing Company, 1995.

Harris, R. Laird. *Leviticus*, Expositor's Bible Commentary, edited by Frank E.
Gaebelein. Grand Rapids: Zondervan Publishing House, 1990.

———. "יַיִן," in *Theological Wordbook of the Old Testament*, edited by R. Laird
Harris. 2:375–76. Chicago: Moody Press, 1980.

Harvard School of Public Health. "Alcohol: Balancing Risks and Benefits."
Accessed April 3, 2014. http://www.hsph.harvard.edu/nutritionsource
/alcohol-full-story.html.

Heintz, Jean-Georges. "בְּאֵר," in *Theological Dictionary of the Old Testament*,
edited by G. Johannes Botterweck and Helmer Ringgren, translated by
John T. Willis. 1:463. Grand Rapids: William B. Eerdmans Publishing
Company, 1977.

Hendriksen, William. *New Testament Commentary: Exposition of the Gospel
According to Matthew.* Grand Rapids: Baker Book House, 1973.

Hingson, R., W. Zha, and E. Weitzman. "Magnitude of and Trends in Alcohol-
Related Mortality and Morbidity among U.S. College Students Ages 18–
24, 1998–2005." *Journal of Studies on Alcohol and Drugs* 16 (July 2009):
12–20.

Holladay, William L. *A Concise Hebrew and Aramaic Lexicon of the Old
Testament.* Grand Rapids: William B. Eerdmans Publishing Company,
1971.

The Holy Bible: 1611 Edition, King James Version. Nashville: Thomas Nelson
Publishers, 1982.

Huey, F. B. *Jeremiah, Lamentations*, New American Commentary, edited by E. Roy Clendenen. Nashville: Broadman Press, 1993.

Hughes, Philip E. *Paul's Second Epistle to the Corinthians*, New International Commentary on the New Testament, edited by F. F. Bruce. Grand Rapids: Wm. B. Eerdmans Publishing Co., 1962.

Hunter, James Davison. *Evangelicalism: The Coming Generation*. Chicago: University of Chicago Press, 1987.

Jaeggli, Randy. *Love, Liberty, and Christian Conscience*. Greenville, SC: Bob Jones University Press, 2007.

Jenson, P. P. "שכר," in *New International Dictionary of Old Testament Theology and Exegesis*, edited by Willem A. VanGemeren. 4:113. Grand Rapids: Zondervan Publishing House, 1997.

Kaiser, Walter C., Jr. *Toward an Exegetical Theology: Biblical Exegesis for Preaching and Teaching*. Grand Rapids: Baker Book House, 1981.

Kent, Homer A., Jr. *Light in the Darkness: Studies in the Gospel of John*. Grand Rapids: Baker Book House, 1974.

Laboratory Equipment. "First Drink Influences Alcoholic Genes." Accessed September 21, 2009. http://www.laboratoryequipment.com/news-drinks -influences-alcohol-genes-092109.aspx.

Lees, Frederic Richard, and Dawson Burns. *The Temperance Bible-Commentary*. New York: Sheldon & Co., 1870.

Lenski, R. C. H. *The Interpretation of St. Paul's Epistles to the Colossians, to the Thessalonians, to Timothy, to Titus and to Philemon*. Minneapolis: Augsburg Publishing House, 1937.

Liddell, Henry George, and Robert Scott. *A Greek-English Lexicon*. London: Oxford University Press, 1925.

Lipinski, E. "סְגֻלָּה," in *Theological Dictionary of the Old Testament*, edited by G. Johannes Botterweck, Helmer Ringgren, and Heinz-Josef Fabry, translated by Douglas W. Stott. 10:148. Grand Rapids: William B. Eerdmans Publishing Company, 1999.

The Literary World: Choice Readings from the Best Books, and Critical Reviews. Review of *The Wines of the Bible: An Examination and Refutation of the Unfermented Wine Theory* by A. M. Wilson. January–June 1877, vol. 56 (vol. 15 New Series), 389.

Longenecker, Richard N. *John and Acts*, Expositor's Bible Commentary, edited by Frank E. Gaebelein. Grand Rapids: Zondervan Publishing House, 1981.

Lumpkins, Peter. *Alcohol Today: Abstinence in an Age of Indulgence*. Garland, TX: Hannibal Books, 2009.

MacArthur, John F., Jr. *Ephesians*. Chicago: Moody Press, 1986.

———. *The MacArthur Study Bible*. Nashville: Thomas Nelson, Inc., 1997.

Masters, Peter. *Should Christians Drink? The Case for Total Abstinence*. London: Wakeman Trust, 1992.

Mayo Clinic. "Alcoholism." Accessed June 14, 2010. http://www.mayoclinic.com/health/alcoholism/DS00340.

———. "Red Wine and Resveratrol: Good for Your Heart?" Accessed October 21, 2013, http://www.mayoclinic.com/health/redwine/HB00089.

M'Clintock, John, and James Strong. *Cyclopædia of Biblical, Theological, and Ecclesiastical Literature*. New York: Harper & Brothers, Publishers, 1891.

McComiskey, Thomas Edward. *The Minor Prophets: An Exegetical and Expository Commentary*, edited by Thomas Edward McComiskey. Grand Rapids: Baker Academic, 1992.

McGrew, Jane Lang. "History of Alcohol Prohibition." Accessed October 24, 2013, http://www.druglibrary.org/Schaffer/LIBRARY/studies/nc/nc2a.htm.

Moo, Douglas J. *The Epistle to the Romans*, New International Commentary on the New Testament, edited by Gordon D. Fee. Grand Rapids: William B. Eerdmans Publishing Company, 1996.

Morris, Leon. *The Gospel According to John*, New International Commentary on the New Testament, edited by F. F. Bruce. Grand Rapids: William B. Eerdmans Publishing Company, 1971.

Motyer, J. Alec. *The Prophecy of Isaiah: An Introduction and Commentary*. Downers Grove, IL: InterVarsity Press, 1993.

Mulligan, Megan K., Igor Ponomarev, Robert J. Hitzemann, John K. Belknap, Boris Tabakoff, R. Adron Harris, John C. Crabbe et al. "Toward Understanding the Genetics of Alcohol Drinking through Transcriptome Meta-analysis." *Proceedings of the National Academy of the Sciences of the United States of America* 103 (16) (April 18, 2008): 6368–73, http://www.ncbi.nlm.nih.gov/pmc/articles/PMC1458884.

National Cancer Institute. "Tobacco Facts." Accessed October 21, 2013. http://www.cancer.gov/cancertopics/smoking.

National Highway Traffic Safety Administration. "Alcohol Impairment." Accessed June 14, 2010. http://www.nhtsa.gov/Research/Human+Factors/Alcohol+Impairment.

National Institute on Alcohol Abuse and Alcoholism. "College Drinking." Accessed October 7, 2013. http://niaaa.nih.gov/alcohol-health/special-populations-co-occurring-disorders/college-drinking.

Nott, Eliphalet. *Lectures on Temperance*. New York: Sheldon, Blakeman & Co., 1857.

NY Newsday. "Sobering Facts on the Dangers of Alcohol." April 24, 2002.

Oswalt, John N. *The Book of Isaiah: Chapters 40–66*, New International Commentary on the Old Testament, edited by R. K. Harrison and Robert L. Hubbard Jr. Grand Rapids: William B. Eerdmans Publishing Company, 1998.

Patton, William. *The Laws of Fermentation and the Wines of the Ancients.* New York: National Temperance Society and Publication House, 1871. Reprint, *Bible Wines or The Laws of Fermentation.* Little Rock, AR: Challenge Press, n.d.

Payne, J. Barton. "Nazirite, Nazarite," in *Zondervan Pictorial Encyclopedia of the Bible*, edited by Merrill C. Tenney. Grand Rapids: Zondervan Publishing House, 1976.

Plutarch. *Plutarch's Moralia in Sixteen Volumes*, translated by Frank Cole Babbitt. Cambridge, MA: Harvard University Press, 1971.

Pliny. *Pliny: Natural History in Ten Volumes*, translated by H. Rackham, in Loeb Classical Library, edited by E. H. Warmington. Cambridge, MA: Harvard University Press, 1968.

Powell, Marvin A. "Metron Ariston: Measure as a Tool for Studying Beer in Ancient Mesopotamia," in *Drinking in Ancient Societies: History and Culture of Drinks in the Ancient Near East*, edited by Lucio Milano. 91–119. Padua, Italy: Sargon srl, 1994.

Quarles, Mike. "Mike and Julia Quarles's Testimony" in *Freedom from Addiction: Breaking the Bondage of Addiction and Finding Freedom in Christ* by Neil T. Anderson, Mike Quarles, and Julia Quarles. 17–193. Ventura, CA: Regal Books, 1996.

Rehm, J., G. Gmel, C. T. Sepsos, and M. Trevisan. "Alcohol-related Morbidity and Mortality." *Alcohol Research and Health* 27 (2003): 39–51.

Reynolds, Stephen M., and Caleb Butler. *The Biblical Approach to Alcohol.* N.p., 2003.

Robertson, Archibald Thomas. *Life and Letters of John Albert Broadus.* Philadelphia: American Baptist Publication Society, 1910.

Rodkinson, Michael L. *New Edition of the Babylonian Talmud*, 2nd ed. Boston: New Talmud Publishing Company, 1903.

Rubini, M. E., C. R. Kleeman, and E. Lamdin. "Studies on Alcohol Diuresis. I. The Effect of Ethyl Alcohol on Water, Electrolyte and Acid-Base Metabolism." *Journal of Clinical Investigation* 34 (March, 1955): 439–47.

Sasson, Jack M. "The Blood of Grapes: Viticulture and Intoxication in the Hebrew Bible," in *Drinking in Ancient Societies: History and Culture of Drinks in the Ancient Near East*, ed. Lucio Milano. 399–419. Padua, Italy: Sargon srl, 1994.

Schaff, Philip. *History of the Christian Church: Ante-Nicene Christianity.* 1910. Reprint, Peabody, MA: Hendrickson Publishers, 1996.

Schreiner, Thomas R. *Romans*, Baker Exegetical Commentary on the New Testament, edited by Moisés Silva. Grand Rapids: Baker Academic, 1998.

Schultz, A. C. "Wine and Strong Drink," in *Zondervan Pictorial Encyclopedia of the Bible*, edited by Merrill C. Tenney. Grand Rapids: Zondervan Publishing House, 1976.

Science News. "Alcohol Answer? Drinks Lower Glucose to Protect Heart." June 30, 2007, 405.

Sidwell, Mark. *The Dividing Line: Understanding and Applying Biblical Separation.* Greenville, SC: Bob Jones University Press, 1998.

Spurgeon, C. H. "The Waterpots at Cana," in *Metropolitan Tabernacle Pulpit: Sermons Preached and Revised by C. H. Spurgeon During the Year 1880.* London: Passmore & Alabaster, 1881.

———, ed. *The Sword and the Trowel: A Record of Combat with Sin and of Labour for the Lord.* London: Passmore & Alabaster, 1877.

Stein, Robert H. "Is New Testament 'Wine' the Same as Today's Wine?" in *Difficult Passages in the New Testament.* 233–38. Grand Rapids: Baker Book House, 1990.

———. "Wine Drinking in New Testament Times," *Christianity Today*, June 20, 1975, 9–11.

Stendebach, F. J. "עַיִן," in *Theological Dictionary of the Old Testament*, edited by G. Johannes Botterweck and Helmer Ringgren, translated by David Green. 11:38–39. Grand Rapids: William B. Eerdmans Publishing Company, 1987.

Stuart, Moses. *Essay on the Prize-Question, Whether the Use of Distilled Liquors, or the Traffic in Them, Is Compatible, at the Present Time, with Making a Profession of Christianity.* Boston: Perkins & Marvin, 1830.

Sunday, William A. *The Sawdust Trail: Billy Sunday in His Own Words*, foreword by Robert F. Martin. Iowa City: University of Iowa Press, 2005.

Tasker, R. V. G. *The Gospel According to St. John: An Introduction and Commentary*, Tyndale New Testament Commentaries, edited by R. V. G. Tasker. Grand Rapids: Wm. B. Eerdmans Publishing Company, 1960.

Teachout, Robert P. *Wine, The Biblical Imperative: Total Abstinence.* N.p., 1983 (based on his doctoral dissertation, *The Use of "Wine" in the Old Testament.* Ann Arbor: UMI, 1979).

Telford, John, and Benjamin A. Barber. Review of *The Wines of the Bible: An Examination and Refutation of the Unfermented Wine Theory*, in *The London Quarterly Review* 49 (October 1877 and January 1878): 220.

Thiselton, Anthony C. *The First Epistle to the Corinthians: A Commentary on the Greek Text*, New International Greek Testament Commentary, edited by I. Howard Marshall and Donald A. Hagner. Grand Rapids: William B. Eerdmans Publishing Company, 2000.

VanGemeren, Willem A. *Psalms.* Expositor's Bible Commentary, edited by Frank E. Gaebelein. Grand Rapids: Zondervan Publishing House, 1991.

Vincent, Marvin R. *Word Studies in the New Testament.* McLean, VA: MacDonald Publishing Company, n.d.

Vos, Geerhardus. *Biblical Theology: Old and New Testaments.* Grand Rapids: William B. Eerdmans Publishing Company, 1948.

Waltke, Bruce K. *The Book of Proverbs: Chapters 1–15*, New International Commentary on the Old Testament, edited by R. K. Harrison and Robert L. Hubbard Jr. Grand Rapids: William B. Eerdmans Publishing Company, 2004.

———. *The Book of Proverbs: Chapters 15–31*, New International Commentary on the Old Testament, edited by R. K. Harrison and Robert L. Hubbard Jr. Grand Rapids: William B. Eerdmans Publishing Company, 2005.

——— and M. O'Connor. *An Introduction to Biblical Hebrew Syntax*. Winona Lake, IN: Eisenbrauns, 1990.

Watts, Robert. Review of *The Temperance Bible-Commentary*, in *The British and Foreign Evangelical Review* 25 (1876): 14.

WebMD. "Driving While Intoxicated: The Facts." Accessed October 17, 2013. http://www.emedicinehealth.com/alcohol _intoxication/page7_em.htm.

West Virginia University, Robert C. Byrd Health Science Center. "Driving and Alcohol." Accessed October 17, 2013. http://www.hsc.wvu.edu/som /cmed/alcohol/driving.htm.

Westcott, B. F. *The Gospel According to St. John.* 1881. Reprint, Grand Rapids: Wm. B. Eerdmans Publishing Company, 1978.

Westminster Review. Review of *The Wines of the Bible: An Examination and Refutation of the Unfermented Wine Theory* by A. M. Wilson. 1877, vol. 108 (New Series, vol. 52), 492–93.

Williams, R. R., and J. W. Horm. "Association of Cancer Sites with Tobacco and Alcohol Consumption and Socioeconomic Status of Patients: Interview Study from the Third National Cancer Survey," abstract. Accessed June 14, 2010. http://www.ncbi.nlm.nih.gov/sites/entrez?Db =pubmed&Cmd=ShowDetailView&TermToSearch=557114&ordinalpos =25&itool=EntrezSystem2.PEntrez.Pubmed.Pubmed_ResultsPanel .Pubmed_RVDocSum.

Wilson, A. M. *The Wines of the Bible: An Examination and Refutation of the Unfermented Wine Theory.* London: Hamilton, Adams & Co., 1877.

Witherington, Ben, III. *Conflict and Community in Corinth.* Grand Rapids: William B. Eerdmans Publishing Company, 1995.

Witmer, J. A. "Review of Robert P. Teachout, *Wine, The Biblical Imperative: Total Abstinence.*" *Bibliotheca Sacra*, 141 (October–December, 1984): 368.

Wood, A. S. "Holiness," in *Zondervan Pictorial Encyclopedia of the Bible*, edited by Merrill C. Tenney. Grand Rapids: Zondervan Publishing House, 1976.

Wood, Leon J. "תָּרַם," in *Theological Wordbook of the Old Testament*, edited by R. Laird Harris. 1:324–25. Chicago: Moody Press, 1980.

Young, Edward J. *The Book of Isaiah: Chapters 40–66*, New International Commentary on the Old Testament, edited by R. K. Harrison. Grand Rapids: William B. Eerdmans Publishing Company, 1972.